ESSENTIALS OF ADVERTISING STRATEGY

SECOND EDITION

DON E. SCHULTZ

STANLEY I. TANNENBAUM

NTC Business Books
a division of National Textbook Company • Lincolnwood, Illinois U.S.A.

1989 Printing

Published by NTC Business Books, an imprint of
National Textbook Company, 4255 West Touhy Avenue,
Lincolnwood, Illinois 60646-1975.

Manufactured in the United States of America.
Library of Congress Catalog Card Number: 87-82610

8 9 0 ML 9 8 7 6 5 4 3 2

Contents

Introduction

Since the first edition of this text was written, advertising, the advertising business, and how we think about advertising has been turned upside down. For all intents, the mass market from and in which most advertising theory was developed is quickly disappearing. *Regionalization, localization,* and even *individualization* are the key terms for the 1990s. Media fragmentation and real-time switching have changed the way we now think about audiences and messages. And, most of all, the consumer and the marketplace have changed, probably forever. Dual-income families, working women, a service economy, and the dramatic increase in the use of sales promotion all have had a major impact on the way we plan and use advertising today.

With all these changes, the demand for sound, well-conceived, effective media advertising is stronger than it has ever been. The need is greater. The risks are greater. And, the resulting rewards are greater for those who can develop and execute measurably effective advertising.

That's what this book is about: how to develop effective advertising. Since the first edition, I've learned a great deal about what makes effective advertising. I've learned from consumers. From students. From consulting projects with major advertising companies and agencies. But in a great measure, I have learned from Stan Tannenbaum. Stan is more than the coauthor of this text. He is a like mind, and, as such, it's almost impossible to tell where my work stops and his starts. As a result, this book is truly the work of both of us. Where credit is due, we have tried to give it. Where there are errors or omissions, they are ours alone.

As always, there are those who should be thanked. Beth Barnes has taken our manuscript, tracked the many illustrations and permissions relentlessly, and been our direct contact with Harry Briggs and his associates at National

Textbook. We also should thank the many advertisers and academicians who have generously granted us permission to use their works as examples of, and in support of, our concepts. Most of all, though, we should thank the students in the Graduate Program in Advertising at the Medill School of Journalism at Northwestern University. Over the years, their insatiable curiosity about what makes good advertising and their challenging questions and discussions within and outside the classroom have done much to force us to think, refine, and re-refine the concepts and approaches found in this text. Much of the work is theirs although our names are listed as authors. Thanks to all of you. And, here's to better advertising.

Don E. Schultz
Evanston, Illinois

Chapter One

The Creative Strategy: Who Needs It?

"What we need is a high-awareness, breakthrough commercial with lots of topspin!" How many times has the desire for creativity been expressed by advertising agency executives? And how is creativity rewarded? Clio, and other top awards given annually for outstanding advertising achievement, are part of the reward system for advertising creativity. (See Exhibit 1-1.)

"What we need is a powerful and compelling commercial with a quick pay-off in sales and profits!" How many times has the desire for effectiveness been promoted by advertisers? And how is this effectiveness rewarded? The cash register, the simplest means of recording sales and storing cash receipts, is part of the reward system for advertising effectiveness. (See Exhibit 1-2.)

Exhibit 1-1 This is CLIO, one of the top awards given every year for advertising creativity.

Exhibit 1-2 Cash register. (Actually, the "Reggie" award given to successful sales promotions.)

The problem is that creativity does not necessarily lead to effectiveness. And effectiveness—measured not in advertising awards, but in sales and profits—is the bottom line. To be sure, there is nothing wrong with advertising that gets noticed. In fact, it is vital. But there is another—even more vital—part of the advertising business. It's the question of how you go about developing breakthrough advertising that meets the advertiser's goals: sales and profits. In our opinion, it really comes down to the "what you say" rather than the "how you say it"—the cash register rather than the Clio. The advertising strategy, the basic ingredient that is the energy of creativity.

Often—*too* often—commercials that are written, accepted, aired, and rewarded are very long on entertainment but very short on salesmanship. A prime example appeared on television several years ago. An award-winning campaign was developed for Piels, a popular regional beer. It featured the cartoon characters Bert and Harry Piel. These two animated spokesmen made TV history with their sophisticated wit and charm. The commercials were the talk of the advertising industry. They were widely quoted and widely imitated. The only problem was that Piel's sales went down, down, down.

The trouble with the advertising was that Bert and Harry charmed everyone in the advertising business. Unfortunately, very few of those who applauded Bert and Harry Piel were beer drinkers. The commercials simply missed the market of beer drinkers who didn't want entertainment but wanted to be told how good the beer tasted.

There must be a balance in advertising between showmanship and salesmanship. One of the purposes of this book is to help bring that balance about.

There are many people in the advertising business today who believe the creative execution alone sells products. They believe the problem with advertising strategies is that they restrict creative thinking and inhibit the creative process. In fact, some creative people claim that advertising strategies are straitjackets that result in square, dull, cookie-cutter commercials or advertisements. These creative people insist that the dullness and sameness of advertising has created an era of *zapping, switching,* and *sleeping.* These are three methods by which people actually cut out commercials when they videotape them; switch away from them via remote control; or, consciously or unconsciously, mentally "turn off" when a commercial appears. We believe that the problem with today's advertising is not so much its monotony and inanity; instead, the problem with advertising is that most ads and commercials are not talking to people's needs and wants. Here's an example.

We've invented a salesman's game called knock-knock. It goes like this. Assume you are a door-to-door salesman and you're out knocking on doors to sell your product. When you knock on a potential customer's door, you're allowed one sentence that will turn your knock into an open door and into a sale. What would you do? Tell a joke? Comment on the weather? Start singing and dancing? Or would you say something meaningful that would solve a problem your prospect might have or satisfy a need or want? For example: "My product can make your home look more beautiful than it's ever been."

The knock-knock, of course, should not—must not—be stated in a dull way. It must come through as a consumer benefit or the door will close in your face, very quickly. And that point applies to ads and commercials as well as to door-to-door selling.

Today, we believe many advertisers and agencies insist on creating advertising without a meaningful knock-knock. Instead, they dwell on fun and games—show business—rather than dramatizing what's in it for the consumer. The benefit. What we call the knock-knock.

To make successful knock-knocks or to make successful ads, you need a disciplined advertising strategy that analyzes the product, the competition, and the consumer, and then logically arrives at a single-minded benefit. The strategy becomes a guide, a road map. And no thinking, imaginative, creative person will reject this type of information and help. On the contrary, a truly creative person will welcome it because it gives him or her insights into the product, the consumer, and the marketplace that will make the creative execution more pointed and far more productive. In fact, many creative people suggest that the tighter and narrower the creative strategy, the more freedom the creative person has. It takes the creative person out of the try everything dilemma and opens up a challenge based on specific information and direction rather than hunches and dreams.

What Is an Advertising Strategy?

A few years ago, *Advertising Age,* one of the leading trade publications, gathered a panel of experts to select the top advertising campaigns of the past 50 years. One of the top vote-getters was the famous campaign developed by Shirley Polykoff, then at the Foote, Cone & Belding advertising agency for Clairol Hair Coloring. (See Exhibit 1-3.)

Many people still remember the theme line "Does she or doesn't she?"

although the campaign started more than 30 years ago. It was a line that shocked some and irritated others but sold like crazy. Clairol's market share shot up in just a matter of months.

The "Does she or doesn't she?" Clairol campaign has often been used as an example of a great advertising strategy. And the overall promotional campaign that Clairol and the Foote, Cone & Belding advertising agency developed is commonly regarded as a strategic marvel. But some people have mistakenly cited the line "Does she or doesn't she?" as the strategic element that made the campaign so successful. The truth is, the strategy was not in the line "Does she or doesn't she?" The true strategy was summed up in the phrase that followed: "Hair coloring so natural, only her hairdresser knows for sure." That's where the real difference in Clairol was summed up for women. The benefit that Clairol offered women who used hair coloring was a product that enabled their hair to look truly natural. No streakes. No unusual tints. No colored look. And the benefits of natural-looking hair that had been colored with Clairol were the strategic consumer-benefit difference that Clairol offered in its product. Certainly, the strategy of natural-looking colored hair did not prevent a brilliant execution. The line "Does she or doesn't she?" got attention and was very persuasive. But the strategy of promising the consumer the benefit of natural-looking hair with Clairol coloring was the real key to success.

"Strategy" and "objectives" and "executions" are some of advertising's current buzzwords. The terms are used, but most often misused by academics and practitioners alike. In order to avoid confusion, here are the definitions we'll use in this text.

Advertising Objective. A clearly stated, measurable end result of an advertising message or messages. Objectives can be measured 1. through actual sales of the product or service; 2. through concrete results, such as the number of coupons returned, telephone calls received, leads generated for the sales force; or 3. in terms of communication effects—that is, changes in awareness, knowledge, preference, or conviction on the part of the target market.

Advertising Strategy. The formulation of an advertising sales message that communicates the benefit or problem/solution characteristics of the product or service being advertised. Strategies are the "what you say" about the product or service. Generally, advertising strategies are developed for use in the mass media.

Does she...or doesn't she?

Hair color so natural only her hairdresser knows for sure!

She's as full of fun as a kid—and just as fresh looking. And this is a lovely thing in a mother! But staying young is not only thinking young, it's *looking* young too. And here, the fresh, young, even color you get *every time* with Miss Clairol, makes the beautiful difference. It's like discovering how to turn back time. It certainly is the best way to keep gray from ever showing.

Keeps hair in wonderful condition— soft, silky. Because Miss Clairol carries color deep into the hair strand, it shines outward with a clear, all-over even tone the way natural color does. That's why hairdressers everywhere recommend Miss Clairol and more women use it than any other haircoloring. So quick and easy. Try it MISS CLAIROL yourself. Today. *HAIR COLOR BATH is a trademark of Clairol Inc. © Clairol Inc. 1964*

Even close up, her hair looks natural. Miss Clairol keeps it shiny, bouncy. Completely covers gray with the younger, brighter lasting color no other kind of haircoloring can promise—and live up to!

Exhibit 1-3 An ad from the Clairol "Does she or doesn't she?" campaign.

Advertising Execution. The physical form in which the advertising strategy is presented to the target market. This generally includes the art, illustrations, words, music, and sound effects that help communicate the advertising strategy to the target audience in order to achieve the advertising objectives. Executions are the ''how you say it'' to your target audience.

In the Clairol example (see Exhibit 1-3), the advertising objective probably was to create awareness, preference, and trial for the Clairol product. The advertising strategy was the promise of natural-looking hair after coloring. The advertising execution consisted of the picture of the beautiful woman, the line ''Does she or doesn't she?'' and the supporting copy and package. Thus, in the Clairol ad, we can see how the advertising execution translates the advertising strategy to achieve the advertising objective.

Our Subject Is Advertising Strategy

This book is about advertising strategy: how to develop strategies, how to select from various alternative strategies, and how to evaluate proposed strategies. But, most of all, the purpose of this book is to give you an understanding of why and how advertising strategy is the key to all advertising successes.

We'll necessarily delve a bit into advertising objectives and advertising executions as we go through the steps in strategy development. Our main thrust, however, will be to illustrate a proven, effective method for developing successful advertising strategies. That goes for everyone. Whether you're a small-town retailer, a major national advertiser, or a beginning student in the field, you can learn to develop effective advertising strategies using the rules and techniques that follow.

Why This Book Is Different

A word of caution. In this text, you won't find many of the subjects that are common to many copywriting or creative books. We won't deal with copywriting or how to structure sentences or create clever phrases. Likewise, you won't find much on layout or art direction. We talk very little about whether you should use color in an ad or whether a particular ad should be a full-page or a quarter-page. You also won't find much about typefaces or arguments for photographs over illustrations. In short, our subject is quite limited but quite clear: This is a book on advertising strategy, the real heart and soul of an advertising campaign and truly the reason why advertising fails or succeeds for any marketer in any marketplace.

What you'll find on the following pages is a very structured approach to developing sound advertising strategies. It's a technique that has been used successfully with all types of products and services, from the largest package-goods advertiser using network television on a regular basis to nonprofit organizations such as hospitals and trade associations. The technique we'll outline has been proven in the marketplace and in the classroom. It works. And it can work for you if you follow the rules we set out.

What Advertising Is All About

Several years ago, Quaker Oats and its agency developed a television commercial for Aunt Jemima Pancake Mix. Although the commercial was written and used to promote Aunt Jemima Pancake Mix, it offers one of the best advertising lessons you'll ever learn.

Look at the storyboard in Exhibit 1-4. It is almost a representation of the knock-knock game presented earlier in this chapter. The salesman is going door to door selling Aunt Jemima Pancake Mix. But what he's really doing is trying to deliver sales messages. That's all selling really is—delivering persuasive sales messages. If the salesperson delivers the right sales message, there's a good chance the prospect will buy. If he or she delivers the wrong sales message or one that is of no benefit to the prospect, the latter probably won't buy. It's that simple. In addition, the Aunt Jemima commercial really shows what advertising is all about, too: delivering effective sales messages to prospective purchasers of a product or service.

Because selling pancake mix door to door isn't very efficient, it's unlikely that any company would try this approach. So, as an efficiency measure, marketers use advertising to deliver sales messages. In other words, advertising is a surrogate for calling on each prospective customer in person and delivering a sales message.

That's the lesson of the Aunt Jemima commercial. Advertising is delivering sales messages to customers and prospects. Marketers can generally reach more prospects more efficiently and often more effectively through advertising than through any other system available, even personal selling, for a wide variety of products and services.

If advertising is simply delivering sales messages, then advertising people must also be salespeople. While advertising may be exciting, glamorous, and

1. (Natural sfx)

2. MAN: Good morning ma'am.

3. This is our Aunt Jemima Buttermilk Complete pancake mix.

4. (Sfx: slam!)

5. Ma'am, our Aunt Jemima Buttermilk Complete...

6. ...has more buttermilk.

7. Makes lighter pancakes.

8. This has more buttermilk than any other mix.

9. Any other. (Sfx: slam!)

10. How do I get to these people? I know.

11. (Sfx: tap, tap) MAN: You can't deny...

12. ...it's a great pancake. (Sfx: slam!)

13. (Natural sfx)

14. WOMAN: What kind of pancake is that?

15. (Anncr VO) Aunt Jemima Buttermilk Complete. You can't deny it's a great pancake.

Exhibit 1-4   Aunt Jemima advertisement

often entertaining, the purpose must always be to deliver sales messages on behalf of the product or service being advertised. That's a concept we'll come back to often in the pages that follow.

The Three Main Rules

There are three main rules for developing effective advertising strategies and effective sales messages for products or services. They apply to every product or service and to everyone who hopes to develop or be involved in effective advertising. They are:

Rule #1: All advertising must take the customer's view.

This simply means that advertising strategies and the resulting advertising executions must always be directed to what the customer or prospect wants to hear or see or is interested in, not just what the advertiser wants to say or do. That's what made the Clairol campaign so successful. "Hair coloring so natural, only her hairdresser knows for sure" was what women were looking for in that type of product. It was the benefit they wanted. And Shirley Polykoff and Clairol were customer oriented enough to know it and to provide it in the advertising.

Rule #2: Advertising is delivering sales messages.

As we illustrated with the Aunt Jemima Pancake Mix commercial, there's really no magic to advertising. It's simply one way a marketer has of delivering sales messages for his or her product or service to a large number of prospective customers in many different locations at the same time. Advertising is nothing more than that. But then, it is nothing less. Thus, if delivery and acceptance of a sales message won't influence the receiver to purchase, then it's unlikely the advertising will be successful, no matter how interesting or entertaining it may be. First and foremost, advertising must persuade. That's the basic premise of a sales message. And persuasion usually occurs when there is a benefit for the receiver, not just for the sender.

Rule #3: Customers buy benefits, not attributes.

Look again at the Aunt Jemima commercial (Exhibit 1-4), particularly at the message the salesman is delivering in the audio. At the first door, he's stressing "Buttermilk Complete pancake mix." That's a knock-knock that fails. At the next house, he's talking about "more buttermilk." Again, no success. And, so on. It is not until he gets to the last house and successfully gets the housewife to taste the product that he generates interest in the product. The reason? People are interested in the taste of pancakes, not in the ingredients or contents of the package. The benefit is the end result the buyer gets. The attributes are those things that make the benefit possible. Consumers are interested in benefits, not attributes. The distinction between attributes and benefits is a key one in developing effective advertising strategies. It's one we'll return to often throughout this book.

Finally, A Word about Creativity

As mentioned earlier in this chapter, what all too often passes for creativity in advertising today has very little to do with presenting a cogent selling message for the product or service. "Creation" means to invent or develop or bring to light something that didn't exist before—to develop a new relationship, a new idea, or a new or unique concept. Something that is creative is new or different or unique. But advertising that is simply innovative isn't necessarily effective in helping motivate customers and prospects to buy. And that, in our view, is the key ingredient. Creativity must provide a new, unique, or more effective way of demonstrating the *benefit* the advertised product or service can provide. It must present the sales message more effectively, not just more dramatically or in a more entertaining way.

The Step-by-Step Approach

To develop or evaluate effective advertising strategies, you must know the basics of advertising. For example, you'll need to know why and how advertising fits into and supports the overall marketing plan. And, if advertising is delivery of a sales message, you'll need to know how people communicate. You'll also need to know how consumers go about making purchasing decisions and how to talk in the language the prospect understands. That's the approach we'll take. All the basics you'll need will be discussed and illustrated.

In the first four chapters, we'll review all the subjects you'll need to know to properly complete our basic advertising strategy form in chapter 5. Following that, we'll take you from advertising strategy to advertising execution in chapters 6 and 7. Chapter 8 is devoted to giving you a method of evaluating advertising executions that others may have prepared from an advertising strategy you developed. In short, the goal of this text is to help you plan and develop more effective advertising.

Chapter Two

From Marketing Plan
to Advertising Strategy

In today's marketing world, a business is generally doomed to failure if it does not look at the product through the eyes of the consumer.

What need does the consumer want to satisfy? What problem does the consumer need to solve? Rather than asking what they can make to satisfy a production problem they have, marketers must look at problems from the consumer's view.

Successful marketing starts with a product that is salable at a price that the right consumer would be willing to pay. Then, the marketer must get it to the marketplace where the customer can buy it. The marketer must promote it— that is, advertise it to convince the consumer to buy it. As you can see, the promotion, in the form of the advertising, is only one part of the marketing program. (See Exhibit 2-1.) And, like the other parts of the marketing program, if it is not done correctly, the whole plan will crumble.

As Exhibit 2-1 shows, a great deal of work goes into the planning, development, and implementation of an overall marketing program before any form of advertising can even be considered. In this chapter, we'll take a look at how the marketing plan determines what the advertising plan can be and how various advertising decisions must be coordinated to support those marketing decisions.

It is important to note at this point that unless the product offers a competitive benefit at a price the consumer is willing to pay—*and* unless the product is in distribution—the greatest advertising plan ever devised will absolutely fail and fail absolutely. In fact, effective advertising will speed the demise of an inadequate product.

Product
Is the product what the consumer wants?
Does it satisfy his needs? Is it better than
competitive products? Does it offer a
competitive consumer benefit? Either
real or emotional?

Price
Is the product competitively priced where
the consumer is willing to pay for it?

Place
Is our product located in a place where it
can be conveniently seen and purchased
by the consumer?

Promotion
Is the competitive benefit of our product
persuasively communicated to the right
consumer?

Exhibit 2-1   The Marketing Mix

Generally, advertising works only when it is combined with effective marketing, and that usually begins when the advertiser listens to the customer. He must determine what product the customer wants and needs rather than what the maker wants to manufacture and distribute.

It is important for the advertising strategist to understand the distinctions between marketing and advertising. It helps prevent overpromise of the advertising results and also insures that there is a sound marketing premise on which to base an advertising strategy.

Effective advertising strategies can only come from effective marketing strategies. Good marketing is always the basis for good advertising.

How Marketing and Advertising Fit Together

Generally, most marketing plans detail how the product or service will be priced, distributed, and promoted. A key element is usually the number of units to be sold and the financial returns from these sales. For most firms, the corporate goal is to make a profit. In the very simplest of terms, the company can generate profits by selling the product for more than it costs to manufacture, distribute, and promote it. To generate greater profits, the company has two choices: 1. reduce costs or 2. generate additional sales.

Most firms commonly have four areas that can be manipulated to increase profits:

1. Product. The product can be changed so that costs can be reduced, or it can be enhanced to make it more competitive, thus generating additional sales volume.
2. Price. The product price can be increased, thus widening the profit margin. Alternatively, the price may be reduced in order to increase volume.
3. Place. Costs can sometimes be reduced by changing the method of distribution of the product. Alternatively, increased product availability or different types of distribution may result in increased sales volume.
4. Promotion. Since most forms of promotion generally require some type of investment by the firm, costs cannot be reduced except by reducing or improving the promotional activity. Therefore, promotional activities are almost always designed to help expand volume.

These elements are commonly called the *marketing mix*. By varying and combining these four factors, marketing managers try to reduce costs and/or increase volume to help meet the corporate goal of increased profits.

For many products and services, particularly those that are broadly distributed and widely used by consumers, the promotion element is vitally important. Promotional activities are generally divided into four basic categories, the combination of which is called the Promotion Mix:

1. Personal Selling
2. Advertising
3. Sales Promotion
4. Publicity/Public Relations

Most companies use some combination of these activities, and the major emphasis is determined by the type of product. For example, major differences in the mix occur for consumer versus industrial products. Higher-priced products generally rely more on personal selling than on advertising. In the distribution system, for example, advertising is generally used for products that are bought over and over through self-service facilities, while products that must be demonstrated rely on personal selling. Thus, the marketing plan generally determines how much advertising will be used and, in some cases, the type of advertising that will be developed.

Can Advertising Solve the Marketing Problem?

Advertising strategists sometimes face an assignment in which advertising simply can't solve the marketing problem. In other words, other elements in the marketing mix are not right or are not coordinated. In such cases, the delivery of a sales message through advertising can't persuade consumers to purchase. Examples are poor product quality, overpricing or a poor price/value relationship, or product distribution that does not allow consumers to find the product. In all these instances, delivering a sales message through advertising probably won't increase sales volume. Thus, any advertising for the product, no matter how strategically correct or well executed, will likely fail to achieve the basic objectives and be considered a failure. For advertising to do its job in the marketing mix, three things must be in place:

1. The product must be right—that is, acceptable in the marketplace to a broad number of prospects.
2. The pricing must be correct. It need not be the lowest price, but there must be a reasonable price/value relationship.
3. Distribution must be adequate. Consumers must be able to find the product if advertising generates interest.

Obviously, other factors may influence the final result, but these three are vital for advertising to have any chance to succeed. The first question you must ask yourself in starting to develop an advertising strategy is, Can advertising help solve this particular marketing problem I have? If it can, proceed. If not, then have the marketing people make the necessary adjustments before you try to develop an advertising strategy.

There Must Be a Product Benefit

Generally, one basic element must be present for any advertising to succeed: The product or service must provide a benefit to the user. If there is no benefit, no advertising, no matter how creative, can be successful.

The product benefit can come in many forms. It can be a direct benefit, such as a remedy that cures a sore throat. It can be an economic benefit, such as a new type of home thermostat that helps reduce home-heating costs. It can be an emotional benefit, such as a bouquet of flowers brought to someone in the hospital. Or it might be a psychological benefit, such as a pair of women's shoes in the latest style. We'll say more about identifying and selecting benefits in chapter 5.

In general, advertising can solve three types of marketing problems:

1. Advertising can provide information about the product, the distribution system, the price, or the benefits that the product might offer. In other words, if elements of the marketing mix are unknown to consumers, advertising can provide information that can solve this type of marketing problem.
2. Advertising can show how the product helps solve a consumer problem. The problem may be obvious, such as how to clean dirty laundry or where to get auto repairs or whom to consult about tax matters. In other cases, advertising can make consumers aware of problems that may not be so obvious. For example, advertising for a telephone answering system points out the problem of not being near the telephone when someone calls. Since the consumer really doesn't know the problem exists, the advertising first calls attention to the latent problem and then provides the solution.
3. Advertising can often solve marketing problems that are caused by mistaken consumer perceptions of the product of the company that markets it. Advertising can be used to help change or clarify perceptions or to improve the image of the marketer.

The key element in the three basic types of marketing problems advertising can solve is the product benefit. It must be in the product or in the advertising. Generally, the benefit forms the basis for the advertising strategy. That's why it is so important to any advertising success.

Competitors and Competition

In almost every marketing plan, one of the essential elements is an analysis of competitors and the competitive situation in the marketplace. The advertising strategist must know and understand the competition that the product faces and the marketing and advertising strategies that these competitors use at every level of competition.

EARTH'S FIRST SOFT DRINK

When the earth was new, mountains rose and valleys were carved and there was created, in what is now called France, a spring that is now called Perrier.*

All the Perrier in the world is born in that spring.

Still clear, pure and sparkling, and minus all those additives that civilization has invented. There's no sugar. No artificial sweetener. No calories. There's no caffeine, no coloring. And Perrier is recommended for salt-free diets, as well.

In modern times, when most beverages are made with water that's been disinfected, softened, oxidated or chlorinated, it's nice also to know that Perrier is naturally filtered as it rises to the surface from its deep underground source.

And so our only concession to civilization is the green Perrier bottle. Because without it, you would never get to enjoy Perrier.

Perrier. Earth's first soft drink.™ Not manufactured, but created by the earth when it was new.

Exhibit 2-2   Perrier advertisement

The four basic levels of competition for a product or service are

1. Desire competition. What type of desire does the customer have or want to satisfy? At any given time, a potential customer's desires can vary from socializing to eating to exercising to traveling and so on. Thus, one of the key competitors for all products is simply the desire the consumer has among all the other possible desires. If the product doesn't solve the desire the consumer has developed, advertising in and of itself can have little effect. Of course, this is a rather broad definition of competition, but it must be considered in selling products. For example, is a candy bar entertainment, eating, socializing, or self-gratification.
2. Generic competition is usually made up of those products or services that can solve the basic desire once it is defined. For example, assume the consumer's desire is to eat. Thus, candy, popcorn, or even rare roast beef would be generic competitors because any or all of them would solve the hunger problem.
3. Form competition consists of the various types of products that might solve the problem. If a person decides to solve her hunger problem by eating candy, then form competitors might be chocolate bars, licorice, or peanut brittle.
4. By far the most common form of competition that advertising strategists consider is brand competition. If, for example, chocolate bars were chosen as the method of solving the hunger desire, then Nestle, Hershey, Mars, and other brands would be in direct competition with one another for the consumer's dollar.

While most advertising strategies are based on providing a method of offsetting direct brand competition, that's not always the case. For example, Perrier advertised its product in the United States not against other bottled waters, but against generic and form competitors, such as liquor, soft drinks, and the like. (See Exhibit 2-2.) Likewise, Kool-Aid seeks to get kids to ask Mom for Kool-Aid rather than carbonated beverages, not just other brands of soft-drink mix. (See Exhibit 2-3.)

The Advertising Plan

To develop a sound advertising strategy, you must look at the whole advertising and promotion picture. That generally comes from the advertising plan. While we won't go into great detail, it will be helpful to review the basic elements that go into most advertising plans. The following outline is a general one that can be used with most products or services.

Exhibit 2-3   Kool-Aid advertisement

I. Executive Summary: One or two pages outlining the basic elements of the plan, the direction, and expected results.

II. Situation Analysis: This section reviews the marketplace situation in which the advertising will be appearing. It generally consists of four sections:

    A. Company and product history

    B. Product evaluation

    C. Consumer evaluation

    D. Competitive evaluation

III. Marketing Goals: These goals generally are drawn directly from the marketing plan and consist of volume, dollar, and perhaps distribution objectives. These are hard measures of what all marketing, not just advertising, efforts are designed to achieve.

IV. Budget: An outline of what is to be spent on advertising with notations, if applicable, for spending restrictions by media or geographic area or for other forms of promotion, such as sales promotion and public relations.

V. Advertising Recommendations: This section can take different forms, but the most common form follows these topics in sequence:

    A. Target market: A description of the persons to whom the advertising will be directed. This should consist of such items as estimated numbers of persons; their geographics, demographics, and psychographics; and their buying and use patterns. (See chapter 10.)

    B. Advertising communication objectives: What the advertising is supposed to achieve. (See the following section in this chapter.)

    C. Creative strategy: This is commonly the advertising strategy.

    D. Executions: The actual form in which the advertising will appear in the media.

    E. Plans: The method by which the advertising will be prepared and the associated costs of producing the specific advertisements or commercials.

VI. Media Recommendations: This section explains how the advertising messages will be delivered to the target market. Commonly four elements are discussed in some detail:

A. Key media problem: Most media plans are built around delivering advertising messages to a specific audience. This section discusses the most difficult delivery problem and how the plan will solve that problem. For example, a major media problem for many advertisers today is trying to reach working women with traditional media. They are not at home during the day, and quite a number of them have very limited media usage patterns.

B. Media objectives: What the media plan is designed to do. Often this is stated in terms of reach, frequency, cost efficiency, time period, and budget level.

C. Media strategy: The general media that will be used—for example, spot television, newspapers, outdoor, and/or radio.

D. Media plans: The specific implementation of the media strategy, including, for example, a list of television stations, magazines, and/or radio stations to be used; an advertising schedule; and the cost.

VII. Sales Promotion Recommendations: Increasingly, the sales promotion program is outlined in the advertising plan. This is done to insure that advertising and sales promotion are designed in concert. Commonly, the four areas discussed cover essentially the same areas that are found in the advertising recommendations:

A. Sales promotion objectives

B. Sales promotion strategy

C. Sales promotion executions

D. Sales promotion plan

VIII. Evaluation: A discussion of how the advertising will be measured. This draws on the Advertising Objectives from Part V-B, above, and describes in detail the steps that will be taken to determine how effective the advertising was in achieving the preset goals. (See the following section in this chapter.)

IX. Conclusions: Generally included here is some type of review that tells why this plan is better than any other plan that might be considered.

As might be expected, advertising plans come in all shapes and sizes and amounts of detail. The above outline could be written in complete detail or could consist of bulleted points and key phrases. Whatever the form, the key elements in the plan for the advertising strategist are:

The Advertising Objectives
The Advertising Strategy
The Advertising Executions

In other words, the strategist must determine what information customers or prospects currently have, what sales messages are to be delivered, and in what form they should be conveyed. These choices are often influenced by available funds, the media that can be used, and the sales promotion activities that are possible in combination with the advertising. While we'd like to think that advertising strategies can be developed exclusively in terms of delivering effective sales messages, the other parts of the overall advertising plan often dictate a general direction to the strategist. We'll see more of this as we start to look more closely at how advertising strategies are developed.

How Advertising Is Measured

There are two basic reasons for developing and implementing an advertising strategy. Obviously, the first is to provide some guidelines for writing the message that is to be developed and communicated. Without a strategy as a guide, creative people have no clear direction as to what is important about the product, why consumers buy or use it, what media they might consider, and the like. The second major reason for an advertising strategy is that it provides a method of evaluating the results of the advertising investment. That's often called accountability, and it is becoming increasingly important in the present era of limited growth, intense competition, and scarce resources.

Within the advertising strategy, the target market is described, the advertising goals outlined, the message to be delivered is spelled out, and the intended results of the advertising are listed. (See chapter 5.) This is the blueprint for

Lavidge & Steiner Model Hierarchy of Effects

Related Behavioral Dimensions	Movement toward purchase	Examples of types of promotion or advertising relevant to various steps
CONATIVE the realm of motives. Ads stimulate or direct desires.	PURCHASE	Point-of-purchase Retail store ads Deals "Last chance" offers Price appeals Testimonials
	CONVICTION	
AFFECTIVE the realm of emotions. Ads change attitudes and feelings.	PREFERENCE	Competitive ads Argumentative copy "Image" ads Status, glamour appeals
	LIKING	
COGNITIVE the realm of thoughts. Ads provide information and facts.	KNOWLEDGE	Announcements Descriptive copy Classified ads Slogans Jingles Sky writing Teaser campaigns
	AWARENESS	

Exhibit 2-4   Lavidge and Steiner model

the advertising program, but the important elements are the goals the advertising is designed to achieve. These are generally listed as advertising objectives.

Advertising Objectives are usually defined in two ways:

1. Whenever possible, advertisers state their objectives in terms of hard measures, such as coupons returned, 800-number telephone calls made, written inquiries received, and bingo cards submitted. These measures indicate the number of specific responses to the advertising.

2. Often, however, the impact of an advertising campaign can't be measured directly in terms of sales or inquiries. That occurs, first, when products are not of great enough interest or concern to warrant additional investigation by the prospect. Few people would go through much of a search to select a brand of popcorn or a can of green beans, for example. Second, it occurs when people are not in the market for or are not able to buy the product when the advertising appears. Few people see an advertisement for an automobile and then rush to the dealer to buy. Thus, the major way advertising is measured is through communication effects. For example, the advertising may create a new or different image in the prospect's mind, which may influence a later purchase; a consumer may make a mental note to try the brand on the next purchasing occasion; or the consumer may simply add the information from the advertising to the base of knowledge that is stored and only called up when a purchase decision is being made. In other words, clear, concise, direct ties between advertising and sales are often difficult to make except in situations in which the advertising is the only selling effort, as is the case in direct marketing.

When we talk about advertising resulting in communication effects with consumers, we generally acknowledge that there is some systematic method or approach that consumers go through in making purchasing decisions. One of the most well-accepted models of that process was developed in the 1960s by Robert Lavidge and Gary Steiner. It is called the *Hierarchy of Effects* model (see Exhibit 2-4) because Lavidge and Steiner proposed that people go through a standard process or series of steps on the way to making a purchase decision. Specifically, they say ''advertising may be thought of as a force which must move people up a series of steps:

1. Near the bottom of the steps stand the potential purchasers who are completely unaware of the existence of the product or service in question.
2. Closer to purchasing, but still a long way from the cash register, are those who are merely aware of its existence.
3. Up a step are prospects who know what the product has to offer.
4. Still closer to purchasing are those who have favorable attitudes toward the product—those who like the product.
5. Those whose favorable attitudes have developed to the point of preference over all other possibilities are up still another step.
6. Even closer to purchasing are consumers who couple preference with a desire to buy and the conviction that the purchase would be wise.
7. Finally, of course, is the step that translates this attitude into an actual purchase.''

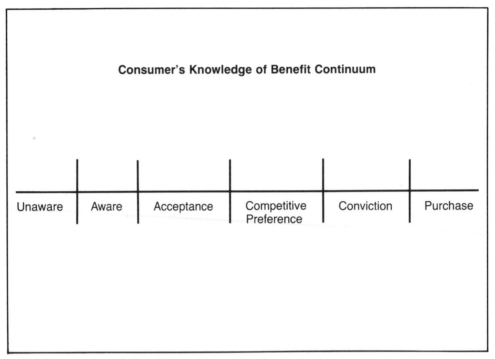

Exhibit 2-5   Consumer's Knowledge of Benefit Continuum

The Lavidge and Steiner (L&S) approach is primarily a psychological model of buyer behavior that has been related to a standard communications model.

Obviously, not all people go through each of these steps in every purchase decision. Yet, the L&S model does provide a good standard for determining the effect of advertising, and a fairly well-accepted method of measuring advertising communication effects has evolved from this model. For example, research is often conducted among consumers to determine what they learned or remembered from the advertising to which they were exposed and what impact those messages may have had on purchasing decisions or intentions.

While the L&S model suggests moving from one level to another, we believe what in fact occurs is that consumers are constantly moving forward and backward along a continuum which leads ultimately to product purchase. We have called this system the ''Consumer's Knowledge of Benefit Continuum'' (see Exhibit 2-5) because as was discussed earlier in this chapter, we believe consumers purchase products only to receive the benefits of those products.

Thus, measuring where a person is in knowing and understanding the benefit makes the advertising that much easier to evaluate.

Whether Lavidge and Steiner's Hierarchy model or our Continuum model is used to evaluate the advertising, the common research methodology is, first, to do a pretest to see what customers and prospects know and how they feel about the product or service before the advertising appears. Then a post-test, conducted after the advertising has appeared, measures changes in awareness, knowledge, and acceptance. The results are used to determine the effectiveness of the advertising approach and content.

Questions

Starting with this chapter, you'll find a series of questions at the end of each major segment in the text—questions that you should be able to answer in order to develop a sound advertising strategy. They are designed as a guide and a checklist. If you can't answer the question for the product or service you will be working with, go back, read the section again, and do some additional digging. You'll need to be able to answer all the questions in order to develop an effective advertising strategy.

1. What is the marketing problem the advertising can solve?
In other words, make sure you are trying to solve an advertising problem and not a major marketing problem. All the marketing mix elements must be in place before advertising can have any effect.

2. What is the product?
You should know not only what the product consists of, what it contains, and how it is made, but also the benefit of having or using it. What is it in actuality? How do people perceive it?

3. Who are the competitors and what kind of advertising are they doing?
Here, you'll have to look at desire competitors, generic competitors, form competitors, and finally, brand competitors. It's important to know what type of advertising they are doing and to speculate on why they are doing it.

4. What are your advertising objectives for this strategy?
To find out if your advertising is working, you must have clearly identified goals and measurement techniques. Determining in advance what your advertising is supposed to achieve can go a long way in helping develop a sound advertising strategy.

5. Can communication of the sales message solve your problem?
If your advertising is eminently successful, will it solve the marketing problem your product or service faces? In other words, is there more to the problem than sim-

ply selecting a target market, developing a sales message, and delivering it to that market? If so, you need to reevaluate your advertising objectives.

It's on to Communication

If advertising is the delivery of a sales messages for a product or service through the media, the next important question is: How do people communicate? That's the subject of chapter 3.

Chapter Three

Communication and Advertising

As we said in the preceding chapter, advertising is simply the communication of a sales message by the marketer about the product or service offered. And the effectiveness of that advertising is often measured in terms of communication effects with the target market.

Communication can be divided into three basic categories:

Individual communication
Interpersonal communication
Mass communication

As the names imply, the processes are primarily identified by the number of persons involved in the communication system and the kinds of channels they use.

Individual Communication

At the individual level, for communication to occur, three actions must take place. First, the receiver must be exposed to the message—in our case, the advertising message. This step is often very complex. In an advertising situation, consumers must avail themselves of the media in which the advertising message appears. Then, they must be exposed to the advertising message. But exposure isn't enough for communication to occur. Next, the advertising must get the consumer's attention. Given the communication noise that generally surrounds most consumers, simply breaking through the clutter is often a difficult task. Finally, the consumer must retain the advertising message. Studies have shown that only about 14 percent of all television commercials are remembered by those who viewed them over the air. Thus, while there may have been high exposure and possibly high attention at the time of viewing, there may have been little retention of the advertising message. In other words, the advertising was not stored in the viewer's memory. Or, if there was some retention, the viewer quickly forgot it. Since memory is limited, all consumers must be highly selective in retaining messages. Thus, advertising that the consumer perceives to have little personal value generally does not result in true communication. The message may be noticed, but it isn't retained over time. We'll see how this storage system works later in this chapter.

Interpersonal Communication

While individual communication generally occurs when a person is exposed to some medium, interpersonal communication occurs when two people exchange information. A model of this face-to-face, or interpersonal, communication system is shown in Exhibit 3-1.

The success of face-to-face communication depends on the sender being able to find or develop some shared field of experience with the receiver. In other words, for communication to occur, there must be words, gestures,

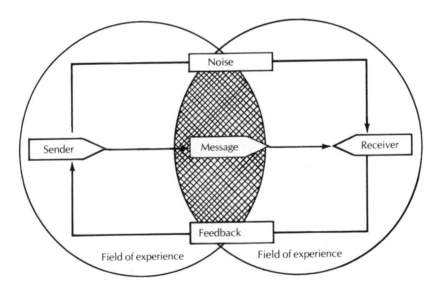

Exhibit 3-1   Face-to-face communication

sounds, or experiences that the sender and receiver have in common. The sender uses these "fields of shared experience" to get the attention of the receiver, to generate interest in the message, and to instill retention of the message.

As shown in the model, there generally is some type of noise in the process. Often, this noise consists of other communications that are going on during the communication process, such as other people talking, dogs barking, and fire engines passing. The message and the shared field of experience must be strong enough to overcome this noise for communication to occur.

Finally, there must be some form of feedback loop in interpersonal communication to enable the sender to know whether or not communication is occurring or has occurred. That feedback can be in the form of verbal agreement, action, or even body language, such as a nod of the head or a smile. No matter how the feedback occurs, the sender generally knows, often immediately, whether his or her message has been received and/or retained by the other person.

An example of how this shared field of experience is used in marketing might help explain the process. Assume you are interested in purchasing a new television set. When you enter the store, the television salesman almost immediately starts to ask you a series of questions, attempting to find a shared field of interest or experience with you. He asks such questions as "Where will you use the new set? What other sets do you have now? Do you want color? and Is remote control important? In the trade, he is said to be "sizing you up." In truth, he's looking for shared fields of experience. If he can find them, he knows he has a better chance of getting his sales message through to you and of convincing you to buy. The same is true in media advertising. The advertiser must quickly illustrate or establish the shared field of interest with the viewer or reader or listener to get attention and to get that person to accept and retain the advertising sales message.

Mass Communication

The major differences between interpersonal communication and mass communication is that in the latter we generally don't know who our audience is, thus making the identification of shared fields of interest difficult, and the feedback loop to the sender is commonly very indirect. Often, the sender has no way of knowing whether the message was received or retained by people in the audience.

If we relate a mass communication model to media advertising, it might look something like Exhibit 3-2. Typically, there are a number of advertisers clamoring for the consumer's attention. All of them are sending persuasive messages through various forms of media in an attempt to influence consumers who expose themselves to the media. As was the case in individual and interpersonal communication, there is noise in the channel and in the system.

Additionally, there is one other factor in the mass communication system: the device people use to control the flow of information to themselves. This is the "screen" called "selective perception." Since memory is limited and the number of messages, events, and noises to which the receiver is exposed is massive, the receiver accepts only those that are of interest to him or her or somehow gain attention. The others are rejected, or screened out.

Once they get past the screen, messages must be decoded. All messages are communicated through a code. That is, colors, sounds, words, pictures, and so on have certain meanings. If the receiver is unable to decode the message or determine these meanings, he or she quickly rejects the communication attempt. Thus, communication cannot occur unless the codes are clear to the receiver. Once the message is decoded, it must be assimilated with existing information or stored as new information. Advertising messages can be acted on immediately, as when a person sees a sign for mints at a candy counter and makes a purchase, or the advertising message can go into memory storage to be used later when a purchasing decision is being made.

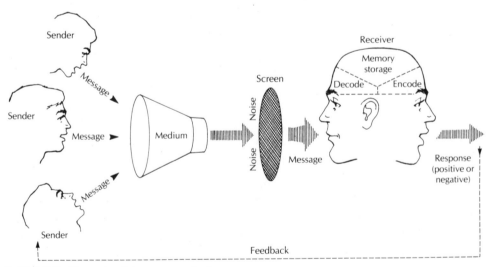

Exhibit 3-2 How advertising communicates

How Advertising Works

In advertising, communication (in any of the methods described above) occurs when the consumer has accepted and internalized the information in some way. How advertising works, then, is very dependent on how the message is accepted, stored, and later used to make decisions. This storage and retrieval system is often based on what we call the *judgment system.*

Judgments are believed to occur as information is processed from the advertising to which the person is exposed. This information is then compared with information the person has previously acquired. In other words, people acquire new knowledge by relating the new information to what they already know.

Three Information Stores

Incoming information, in the form of advertising or any other sensory activity, passes through or is subject to three information store systems.

The first step is to the sensory register (SR). (See Exhibit 3-3.) It has three purposes. First, all incoming information, either auditory or sensory, is transduced so that patterns can be recognized. For example, the SR detects forms (letters such as B or Z), sounds (such as "Ah" or "Ouch"), and shapes (such as balls or circles or figures). It then holds the information for later processing. Finally, it alerts higher brain centers so they can process the information.

The second stage is the short-term memory store (STS). Information is held temporarily in STS while reasoning takes place and judgments are made. Because STS is *active* memory, it has a very limited capacity.

The third stage is the long-term store (LTS). This is the repository of all information that a person has ever processed. The LTS holds information that is currently not being used. Long-term memory is organized in two ways so it can be retrieved. First, there is a semantic organization, which is believed to be hierarchical. For example, if a person is thinking of the cookie category, the first level might be the various forms of cookies, such as hard or soft, large or small, and filled or unfilled. At the next level might be flavors of cookies, such as chocolate chip, vanilla wafers, or coconut macaroons. At the bottom might be brands of cookies, such as Keebler, Grandma's, or Duncan Hines. In addition, at each level, other factors, such as color, time of use, method of purchase, or even cost might be associated.

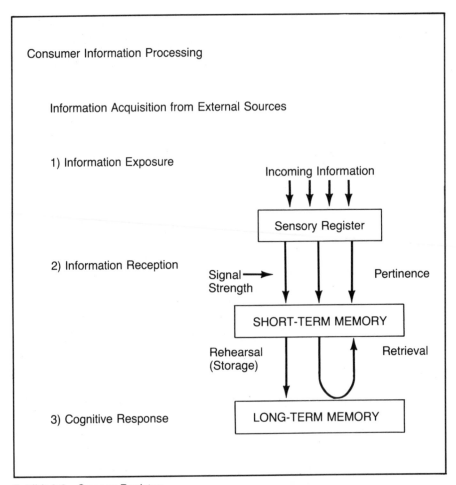

Consumer Information Processing

Information Acquisition from External Sources

1) Information Exposure

2) Information Reception

3) Cognitive Response

Exhibit 3-3   Sensory Register

The second way information is stored is temporally. In other words, people store information in the order in which events or activities have occurred over time. Thus, people can recall their lives in the order in which they experienced events or can recall experiences with products or even advertising messages from times long past.

Retrieval, Storage, and Representation

Let's assume a person is watching television and sees a commercial. The information presented is in the SR. If the commercial is not processed further, there will be no recall of the message. It simply passes away.

If the commercial is processed, the person becomes aware of it and several responses are possible. One is not to devote further processing to the commercial. If this occurs, there will be little recall of the message at a later time. If, however, the person decides to activate information previously stored in LTS, a process called *retrieval* occurs. In other words, the person decides that the new information is worthwhile or interesting enough to call up previously stored information for comparison.

When that comparison is made—that is, when the person relates the new information in the commercial to previously stored information from LTS, the process is called *rehersal*. Based on comparison of the new information in the commercial in STS with previously stored information from LTS, he or she makes a judgment. This judgment can be acted on immediately or may go back to LTS to be called up again and reconsidered.

As shown in Exhibit 3-3, two factors often impact on the sensory register, which determines whether or not material goes to short-term memory: signal strength and pertinence. Signal strength can range from the scream of a child in pain to the hum of a bee in summer. It also can relate to the number of times the advertisement or commercial has been seen before. Pertinence is based on how the person's experiences have been formed and the interest the person has in the subject from which the information comes. There must be a strong signal, and the message must be pertinent enough for the receiver to go through the judgment process.

In summary, judgments are made in the following way. First, information presented in advertising is represented in the SR. The SR holds the information for further processing and interprets the characteristics of the stimulus. If the signal in the form of advertising is sufficiently strong and pertinent to the person, it calls forth information that has been held in long-term storage. This enables the new information in the advertising to be brought to short-term storage and processed and then stored again.

From this description, we can see that there are several important factors in the development of effective advertising strategies. Two come to mind immediately. First, the information contained in the advertising must be strong enough and pertinent enough to be considered for further processing. If the information is too weak or too irrelevant, the advertising has no chance of having an impact. Second, advertising must be consistent enough so that it will be accepted when judged against information previously processed and held in long-term storage. If, for example, the advertising says that hot coffee is a good beverage for a very hot summer day, it is likely that this message will not square with information people have stored about summer drinks or

Exhibit 3-4   Wrigley's Spearmint Gum advertisement

the use of coffee. Exhibit 3-4 is more likely to mesh with a consumer's view of fun in the summertime.

Questions

Before going further, you should be able to answer the following questions about the product or service for which you are developing an advertising strategy.

1. What fields of knowledge do you share with consumers?

In other words, can you empathize with the persons to whom the advertising is being directed? Do you know how consumers use your product or service? How they feel about your brand? Here, it is best to think of one single person who represents the group you want your advertising to reach, rather than a faceless mass.

2. Where does the consumer stand on knowledge of your benefit?

How much do consumers know about the category, the product, and the brand? Are they aware of your brand? How many like or prefer your brand? It's important to have some idea of how many persons are at what point on the benefit continuum so you can develop a strategy that helps move them forward.

3. How important is your product or service to your target market?

Remember the importance of pertinence to the consumer in simply getting your message into STS. If your product is of minor interest, you will have to find benefits that make the product more important in order for consumers to pay any attention to the advertising.

4. What kind of response do you expect this advertising to generate?

Judgments are the key. What judgment do you want receivers of your message to make? Should they leap from their chairs, rush to the nearest store, and purchase immediately? Or are you trying to change a misperception about the quality of the product or the price/value relationship? It is vital that you have a clear idea of what your target market is supposed to do as a result of seeing and processing your advertising.

With this view of communication, the next step is to understand a bit about how consumers behave in the marketplace. That is the subject of the next chapter.

Chapter Four

How Consumers Make Purchasing Decisions

Having looked at communication and at how consumers accept, process, and store information, we should now investigate how consumers use the advertising information to which they are exposed or which they seek out to make buying decisions. There is still considerable controversy among researchers on exactly how consumers behave in the marketplace, that is, how they make purchasing decisions. This is partly because we still don't fully understand human nature, but it also stems from the question of whether buyers of industrial products such as incinerators, chemicals, or steel plating follow the same patterns as do consumers shopping for personal needs. The behavior patterns we describe below primarily reflect the method in which widely available, low-risk, frequently purchased products are chosen. It can be applied to other product categories in developing advertising strategies.

Needs and Wants

All product- or service-purchasing decisions made by consumers are based on satisfying either a want or a need. Needs are generally defined as those things that are necessary for survival, that is, food, water, clothing, shelter, and safety. Wants are things that consumers desire but aren't necessarily life sustaining. Examples might include cosmetics, sporty automobiles, compact discs, and oriental rugs.

Today, in the United States, most of the basic consumer needs are satisfied in some manner. Granted, there are people whose basic needs are not satisfied, but most of the population is seeking to satisfy wants. Thus, most adver-

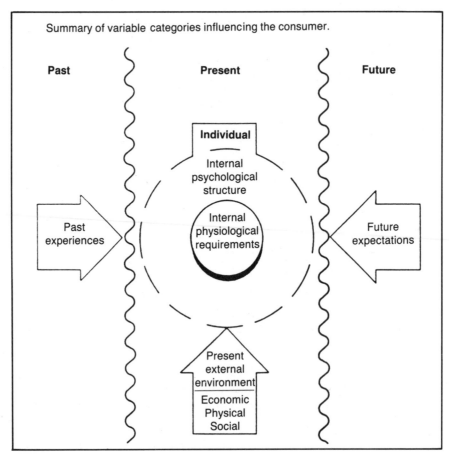

Exhibit 4-1   Decision variables

tising is for products that supply want satisfaction rather than need satisfaction. That's clear from the advertising expenditure charts. They continually show the major advertisers to be companies that manufacture or process automobiles, beer, detergent, and cosmetics. In developing an effective advertising strategy, you should understand that the product with which you are working generally satisfies wants rather than real consumer needs.

Consumer behavior specialists often describe wants and needs either as *active* or *latent*. Active means the consumer recognizes the need or want and actively seeks to satisfy it. For example, an active need might be for a heavy winter coat. Thus, the consumer will scan newspaper or magazine advertisements, visit shops or stores, or leaf through catalogs seeking the best offering. On the other hand, a latent want or need is generally something that doesn't have high priority in the consumer's life. In fact, the want might not even be recognized by the consumer until it is called to his or her attention through some form of advertising. Examples of products that have been developed to solve latent needs are panty hose, frozen food, luxury cruises, and instant coffee.

In an attempt to understand how consumers make product and brand purchasing decisions, we generally describe the decision process as either rational or emotional. Rational decisions are those in which the consumer consciously considers various alternatives and attempts to determine the best price-value relationship. In rational decision making, the consumer may take into account several factors. For example, the purchases of products such as refrigerators or television sets or services such as colleges or universities are commonly based on rational decisions. Emotional decisions are made primarily to enhance the self-image of the consumer. Examples in which emotional decision making is used might include such items as cosmetics, greeting cards, fashionable clothing, and even automobiles.

To plan an effective advertising strategy, you must understand how your product fits into the life of your prospective purchaser or user. You must know whether the need or want your product or service can satisfy is one that is actively sought by prospects or is a latent desire that you must develop. Equally important, you must determine whether the decision process you are attempting to influence is rational or emotional. If it is a rational decision, a well-supported, logical, value-oriented strategy probably would be best. If it is an emotional decision, images, icons, and even relationships with other products or people may form the basis for the strategy.

How Consumers Make Purchasing Decisions

Once we understand the needs and wants of consumers and how our product or service might satisfy them, the next step is to look at the process consumers go through to make a purchasing decision.

First, it is important to understand that consumer purchasing decisions are very complex, and they are influenced by a number of factors. Exhibit 4-1 illustrates one concept of these decision variables.

As Exhibit 4-1 shows, the individual is at the center. Within the individual are his or her internal physiological requirements. We earlier referred to many of these as basic needs. In addition, there is a basic internal psychological structure, which includes the person's subjective knowledge, values, and beliefs. These commonly determine wants.

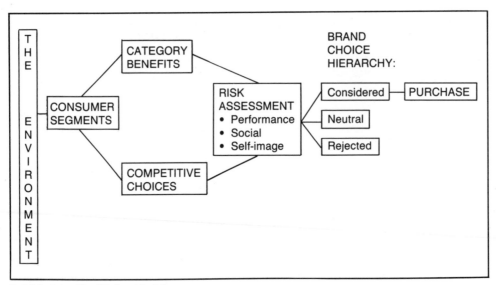

Exhibit 4-2 The Pitcher Model

The external environment is capable of influencing the individual's psychological condition and therefore his or her behavior. There are three aspects of the environment. The first is the present—the physical, economic, and social situation in which the consumer finds him- or herself at the present time. The second aspect is the past—all the ideas, concepts, and situations that the person has stored over time about a product or service, including personal experiences, comments of friends or relatives, and previous advertising. The third factor is the future—things that consumers expect to occur, such as changes in income, health, and job security.

One of the key determinants in consumer decision making is the interaction among and influence of these variables. Some factors may well influence other factors or may even cancel out others. In short, the consumer decision-making process is both complex and dynamic. It is this dynamism, coming from the constantly changing variables inside and outside people, that makes the development of an advertising strategy such a challenging task.

A fairly well-accepted model of the steps consumers go through to make a purchase decision is illustrated in Exhibit 4-2.

In the model (where the consumer moves from left to right), consumers initially segment themselves within the environment—or, in advertising, within the marketplace. This generally comes about through product or service usage. Thus, the consumer segments him- or herself into such groups as tuna fish users, smokers, mothers, or long-distance telephone callers. This self-segmentation by the consumer is vital to the advertising strategist because these segments identify the basic need or want consumers are seeking to satisfy.

Once this basic segmentation has occurred, the consumer generally evaluates potential products or brands in two ways. The first is based on the category benefits that various products provide. For example, assume a consumer has $3,000 in discretionary income available. The first step might be to choose the category in which to use those funds. Alternatives might be recreation, self-improvement (education), transportation, home improvement, or clothing. Assume, for this example, that our consumer chooses recreation. Once in that category, the choices become quite wide. She could 1. take a cruise, 2. go skiing, 3. buy an outdoor swimming pool, 4. go camping, 5. take a bus trip to New York City. These alternatives make up the competitive choices that are available. The consumer makes her choice based on the category benefits that are considered and evaluated. Thus, the cruise might offer sun, swimming, good food, and companionship. The swimming pool might offer ongoing entertainment, enhancement of the home, and enjoyment for the family and neighborhood. The consumer's choice is commonly based on a risk assessment of the alternatives.

Risk Assessment is generally based on three qualities either real or perceived by the consumer. The first is performance, that is, how well the consumer thinks the alternative being considered will perform based on her expenditure of time or money. The second is social risk, or how well the choice will be accepted by one's mate, family, social circle, or even society in general. The third is self-image. This simply means how well the alternatives fit with the person's image of herself. For example, the consumer might consider herself to be the type of person who goes on cruises but doesn't go camping. Cruising is neat, fun, and upscale while camping is cold, damp, and dirty. Thus, our consumer might believe that camping would lower her self-image, while cruising in the South Seas might enhance her self-image.

Having made the category choice and the initial risk assessment, the consumer then starts to evaluate various brand alternatives. In this instance, assume the choice was made to take a cruise. While a number of factors would obviously be included in the decision choice, such as length of cruise, cruising area, embarkation point, and the like, the choice often comes down to a brand choice.

Let's assume our consumer has narrowed the choice down to seven-day cruises in the Caribbean. Some of the cruise lines that serve this area are Cunard, Royal Viking, Carnival, and Royal Caribbean. Let's further assume our consumer is somewhat knowledgeable about cruising and has had some experience. She has sailed aboard Cunard and has friends who have been on Royal Viking cruises. Assume further that she has heard of Carnival Cruises and has the impression that Royal Caribbean cruises are very expensive. She might then group her brand choice hierarchy into 1. Considered: Cunard and Royal Viking, 2. Neutral: Carnival, and 3. Rejected: Royal Caribbean, because of her impression of the high cost and her limited funds. Ultimately, from the set of two brands she considers, she selects Royal Viking.

Obviously, the same sort of risk assessment—that is, of performance, social, and self-image risks—is made of the cruise line alternatives as was made with the category choice. In most instances, this risk assessment actually determines the brand choices that are considered.

While this example of consumer decision making is highly simplified, it does illustrate the basic steps that consumers commonly use. Furthermore, it illustrates when and how advertising may have some impact in the decision process. The major points of opportunity for advertising would be in 1. Category Benefits, 2. Competitive Choices, and 3. Risk Assessment. In developing an advertising creative strategy, one must determine which of these three decision points the advertising is designed to influence. Further, it becomes clear there are differing tasks for advertising depending on where the advertising planner believes the consumer can be most clearly influenced.

Some Additional Consumer Behavior Concepts

Evolving from the model in Exhibit 4-2 are two important concepts in advertising strategy development.

The first is the concept of high and low involvement. One major concept in consumer behavior is that consumers are either greatly or highly involved in the decision process, or they devote little attention to the brand choice and thus have low involvement. Simply put, involvement theory has to do with how much time, effort, and attention consumers devote to the selection of the category, product, and brand. In the case of an ocean cruise, it would seem quite logical that the consumer would be highly involved in the choice of the cruise line. This choice is a high-risk, relatively expensive, and high-visibility decision. Alternatively, the theory goes, one is less involved in the selection of a brand of green beans. Most consumers see little risk, either financial or social, in the brand choice, and many probably believe one brand of green beans will taste as good as another. Thus, one of the considerations of the advertising strategist is the involvement of the consumer with the prod-

Indicators of High-Involvement Brand Choice	Determinants of Low-Involvement Brand Choice
1. Information seekers/processors	1. Information gathered at random
2. Active audience	2. Passive audience
3. Evaluate brands	3. Buy first, then evaluate
4. Maximize satisfaction	4. Acceptable level—no problems
5. Personality, life-style, and reference groups strongly influence	5. Little personality, life-style, or reference group influence

Exhibit 4-3   High and low involvement

uct and the brand to be advertised. High involvement might suggest one strategy approach, while low involvement might suggest another.

As a guide, a comparison of high versus low involvement is shown in Exhibit 4-3.

The second concept is that of the Evoked Set. This refers to the brand choice hierarchy in the Pitcher model (Exhibit 4-2). The idea supporting evoked set is that most consumers generally consider one or more brands acceptable. For example, in the cruise choice above, the consumer's evoked set consisted of four brands, of which two were considered.

Still another way of looking at the consumer's involvement with product categories is along the purchase continuum, which we mentioned in chapter 2. Consumers care first about "What's in it for me?" when they consider a product category and a brand within it. (See Exhibit 4-4.) However, when the involvement or risk with the product is low, as in a product such as Lifesavers, they merely need to be aware of the benefit of the brand. If the involvement is a little more important, as in green beans, they might have to be somewhat persuaded that the benefit is for them. In the case of a car or a cruise, a comparison of benefits is normally demanded. However, in the purchase of a car the comparison may be cursory because of time, distances, and emotional involvement. But with a cruise decision, it is conceivable that a new prospect with no past experience may spend months studying brochures, talking with past users, and even visiting a boat. (See Exhibit 4-5.)

When only one brand is known or considered, the consumer is said to be *brand loyal*. Not considering other choices, the consumer continually buys

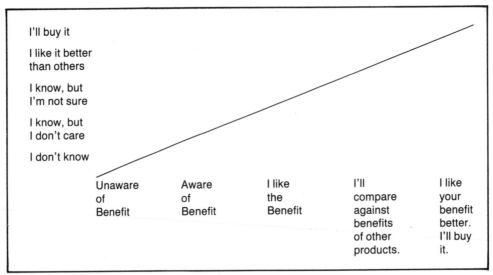

Exhibit 4-4 The "What's in it for me?" curve

the same brand again and again. Increasingly, however, fewer and fewer consumers are brand loyal in any category. There is simply too much advertising and promotion, too many product alternatives, and too many shopping choices for a consumer not to consider more than one product before making a purchase. In our cluttered marketplace, several brands are often brought to mind when a purchase is considered. Thus, in many instances, the goal of such advertising is simply to make the brand acceptable—that is, to be a considered choice and a member of the consumer's evoked set.

Brand Choice Influences

Flowing directly from the idea of a brand choice hierarchy are factors that commonly are used by consumers to evaluate particular brands in a category. While the following list is not all-inclusive, it will illustrate some of the more important factors the advertising planner must consider in developing an advertising strategy.

1. Past Experiences. As we saw in the cruise line example, a major factor in the consumer's brand decision was the experience the prospect had with the cruise line. Given a pleasant experience or satisfaction with the brand in the past, the consumer is certainly likely to consider the

	Unaware of benefit	Aware of benefit	After some thought benefit seems good to consumer	Consumer still needs more information to be convinced	Consumer must compare competition	I'll buy it
Lifesaver mints						
Green Beans						
35 mm camera						
Car						
Cruise						

Exhibit 4-5 The benefit continuum, as applied to various product categories

same brand on the next occasion. The reverse is also true. It is extremely difficult to overcome a bad product experience. In most cases, it is almost impossible for advertising to accomplish this task.

2. Price. The second most important brand choice influence is price. In most consumer studies, price is the dominant factor consumers use in making a choice among considered brands. In many cases, the task of advertising is either to improve the perception or actual price of the brand in comparison with alternatives.

3. Situation. The situation in which the purchaser finds him- or herself or the situation for which the product is purchased has a major impact on the brand decision. For example, brand choices often change when a person is shopping with a friend or when buying a gift for a relative. In addition, the consumer also finds himself in a changing situation. For example, a substantial salary increase often influences the choice of brands. And the reverse is often true when a person is unemployed for a long period of time or in an unfamiliar shopping situation.

4. Product Importance. The importance of the product or service to the consumer is also a factor in brand decisions. For a young woman, dress and clothing are very important. They are generally less so for women living in retirement. Thus, brand choice and visibility of the brand selected is key to the first group, while it is relatively unimportant to the second. Consumers often attach varying levels of importance to products and services depending on their particular life-style.

5. Product Differences. All marketers would like to think that their products are dramatically different from, and perhaps better than, their competition. Unfortunately, in today's marketplace, real or meaningful product differences are increasingly difficult to find. When there are

major product advantages, such as those Polaroid cameras or
Macintosh computers have over competition, consumers are quick to
accept them as a reason for making a brand choice. In these cases, the
development of the advertising strategy is quite straightforward.
However, it is not so simple a task when there are no meaningful
differences in the product or service. Yet, parity products are generally
the most highly advertised. Thus, the advertising strategist must be
very skilled in developing a plan for these kinds of products.

6. Perceptions. In the absence of product differentiation in today's
   marketplace, that is, with products at parity, advertisers attempt to use
   product perceptions as a meaningful way for consumers to decide
   between brands. Through advertising, marketers hope to convince
   consumers that it is not so much what the product really is, as how it is
   perceived, that separates one product from another. For example,
   consumers who generally couldn't differentiate between brands are
   encouraged to select one over another because it is used by a film star
   or a sports hero. Thus, the product is perceived as having more status
   or prestige than a competitor, and that element is used by consumers to
   make a brand choice.

The advertising strategist will undoubtedly find a number of other factors
that can influence a consumer's brand choices in particular product or service
categories. These factors, however, are generally common across categories
and illustrate the principle.

Clustering Consumers: Developing Target Markets

Earlier, we said that consumers usually segment themselves from the general environment by their wants and needs. Often, this categorization occurs
in the mind of the consumer and is thus difficult for the advertiser to know or
understand. To assist in developing an effective advertising strategy, advertisers engage in a common technique called *target marketing* by directing
their advertising to a cluster of consumers or a target market. In essence, it
means identifying a group of consumers out of the total population who seem
to have something in common and then to aim the advertising toward them.
While there are many ways to group or cluster consumers, the ones listed
below are the most frequently used.

1. Geographics. People who live in certain geographic areas often have
   common needs—for example, antifreeze in northern Minnesota,
   swimsuits in Florida, chili peppers in Texas and New Mexico, and

briefcases in Washington, D.C. By looking at geographic usage of products or services, the advertiser is often able to isolate particular areas of the country in order to address its advertising to the common needs and wants of large numbers of consumers.

2. Demographics. The most commonly used variable in developing target markets is demographics. These are measurable facts about consumers that provide some distinguishing characteristic. Examples are age, sex, income, home ownership, education, marital status, and number of children in the home. While these categories are very broad, they do help to identify certain market characteristics. For example, unmarried or childless couples generally have little interest in children's clothing, and most younger people have little category or brand interest in investment plans.

3. Psychographics. Often termed *life-style variables*, these are commonly internal, psychological factors that consumers use to distinguish themselves from others—the way they perceive themselves and how they fit in society. Often, these factors determine how a consumer will spend his or her income and the brands he or she will buy. While two male heads of household may be the same demographically—in terms of age, income, marital status, number of children, and so on—the psychological differences between a radio disk jockey and an accountant can be dramatic when it comes to selecting an automobile. Increasingly, psychographic factors are the determining influence in consumers' brand choices. That's why the product or service image portrayed by advertising is so important to the success of the product in the marketplace.

4. Media Patterns. The media to which consumers expose themselves has much to do with the success of the advertising reaching and influencing them. Thus, the advertising strategy developer should look not just at what advertising medium he or she wishes to use; instead, he or she must look at what media the target group uses. With the fragmentation of the media audience, the use of media patterns becomes increasingly important in the success of an advertising strategy.

   One prime example of the importance of media patterns can be found in selling to working women. Since these consumers are out of the home most of the day, traditional daytime television is ineffective. Increasingly, therefore, advertisers are turning to early morning and late afternoon radio, late night television, and magazines to reach this growing market.

5. Usage Patterns. As the Pitcher model (Exhibit 4-2) showed, the prime factor influencing brand choice is simply product category usage. For example, there is little potential for cigarette sales among nonsmokers, but advertising can influence a brand switch among smokers. Thus, knowing what brand, when, and how much the prospect uses is vital to the advertising strategist.

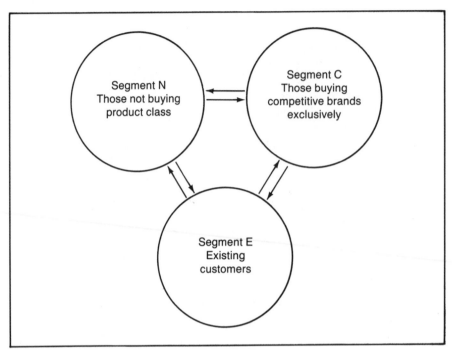

Exhibit 4-6   Where do customers come from?

One of the most useful tools in developing an advertising strategy is the simple chart in Exhibit 4-6, within the framework of which will be found the entire market for any product or service under any conditions at any given time.

The entire marketplace for the product is contained within Exhibit 4-6. Of the three groups, those in the circle labeled N are nonusers in the category. In other words, they either do not now or have never used a product in the category. Thus, while they may become users, at this time they are not. The objective of advertising would then be first to turn them into category users.

Those in group C are product users, but they favor competitive brands. The goal of advertising to this group would likely be to get them to either switch or try the advertiser's brand. Thus, the advertising strategy would most likely stress competitive benefits or reasons why the advertised brand is better in some way.

The third group, group E, includes existing customers of the advertised brand or those who primarily buy the advertiser's brand. The advertising strategy to this group would generally be to reinforce their brand decision. The advertising would support the decisions they had already made and confirm that the brand choice was right for them.

One notable aspect of the model is that arrows flow both in and out of each group. This denotes the dynamism of the marketplace. That is, consumers are constantly making brand decisions and moving either in or out of the category or between brands. Today's existing customer may well switch to a competitor's brand tomorrow and vice versa. The advertising strategist must constantly keep in mind the target market he would like to influence, its category, and its brand usage in order to determine what type of messages might be most appropriate.

One Common Denominator: What People Buy

While we have taken a brief but thorough look at how consumers make purchase decisions and at some of the factors that influence those decisions, one thing must be stressed:

CONSUMERS BUY FOR ONLY ONE REASON: TO FIND
SOLUTIONS TO PROBLEMS THEY EITHER HAVE OR
PERCEIVE THEY HAVE

One of the most common mistakes advertisers make is to believe that consumers buy for the same reasons they want to sell—that is, because of product differences, lower price, inherent quality, or some other competitive factor. In truth, most consumers buy only to solve a problem they think they have or to prevent a problem from occurring. Thus, consumers look at solutions to problems, not at product ingredients, construction, or even price as a method of selecting products or services. An example might help: "Consumers want to buy quarter-inch holes; they don't want to buy quarter-inch drills."

It is the benefit the product or service provides that consumers want, not the attributes that make the benefits possible. Consumers are interested in the sound coming from a stereo system, not the woofers, tweeters, or stylus used in the set. They are interested in the speed and ease of calculations and word processing that computers offer, not the RAMs, ROMs, and bytes. Or they are interested in how effectively a bug spray kills bugs, not what the active ingredients are.

In planning an advertising strategy, keep this always in mind: Look at your product or service from the view of the consumer. What does the consumer want the product to do or what problem can it solve? Sell the benefits of the product. Use the attributes to support why those benefits are possible.

With this view of consumer behavior, we now move to the actual development of an advertising strategy in the next chapter.

Questions

Before you move on, however, you should be able to answer these questions about your product or service:

1. Will the product or service fill a want or a need?

More than likely, you'll be advertising to fill a want. If so, how important is that want in the consumer's life? To get attention, you must have something that breaks through all the other choices the consumer has to make each day.

2. What product or service perceptions now exist?

Unless your product or service is totally new on the market, many of your customers and prospects have some idea of what your product and brand is and how it fits into their lives. To develop a winning strategy, you must consider what is already known or accepted or perceived about your product.

3. What are the category benefits?

There are inherent benefits in any product category. What are they? How well does your product live up to these accepted norms? Are you better than, the same as, or worse than the competition? Will you have to build new benefits into your product to be on a par with competition?

4. Is there any risk involved with your product?

All products and services have some sort of risk. These may include those shown in the model—such as performance, social, or self-image risks—but there are others. For example, how much time is required to learn how to use or operate your product? What is the actual out-of-pocket financial risk? What about the risk of changing from a known and well-used brand? All these must be considered.

5. Is the product or service in the consumer's evoked set?

Is your brand one that is commonly considered when a purchase decision is being made, is it neutral, or, heaven forbid, is it simply rejected out of hand? Depending on how your product stands with consumers, you can determine your strategy and whether you are seeking to build brand loyalty or trying to make the brand acceptable.

6. What consumer segments exist now?

Before you start trying to segment the market or to determine target markets, make sure you know what natural markets already exist or how competitors may have already segmented the market. To compete in a marketplace, you must know how both consumers and competitors operate, and structure that into your thinking.

Chapter Five

How to Develop a Creative Strategy

Knock-knock. The door opens. The woman behind the door frowns. The salesman says, "You should buy this product because it'll make your life easier." The woman says "Come on in, show me." And the salesman is on his way to a sale.

This concept of knock-knock—"here's what my product will do for you"—is really what is behind the ideal creative strategy statement. Some agencies and advertisers insist on strategies that list vague advertising objectives, like building awareness and favorable attitudes, describing the vital signs of the presumed target customer (2.1 children, 8 dogs, etc.), and setting down the main product features to communicate. Although this type of strategy may have brevity on its side, it certainly gives the creative person only a superficial feel for the product, the customers, and the marketplace.

What salesman can do a proper selling job if he doesn't know the product inside and out, including how it is perceived by prospective customers? And the salesman must know his competition as thoroughly as he knows his own products. Who are you really competing against? Is it a product similar to yours or is the competitive brand much broader? What are the strengths of the competition? Their weaknesses? The perception of them in the market? Who is the most vulnerable? From whom will you take business?

And what good salesman ever tried to make a sale before he sized up his customer? What does the prospect need from the product category? What does he want from the product category? How does he live? Shop? How will he use the product? Why? When?

A salesman on the retail floor or going from door to door takes all these questions into consideration and then decides what competitive benefit will get the customer to buy. And, importantly, he will also decide on the most effective way to deliver that benefit.

That's what an effective creative strategy is all about. It is simply a proven way to formalize a salesman's thinking process. It is a selling strategy. Its effectiveness is enhanced because by using the form given in this book, you can put it down on about one-and-a-half sheets of paper. Thus, it will be easily read, digested, and used by the client and every concerned party at the agency.

The strategy will serve as a road map for the advertiser and for all the service departments of an agency. It serves as a fund of knowledge for the creative person. It tells him what the product is, who the consumer is who the competition is and what it is doing, and which competitive benefit to offer that customer and the support needed to make the benefit believable. In our opinion, the strategy statement is not a straitjacket. It is a thinking process that leads to a creative execution with substance rather than fluff. Some of the finest creative people hail it as an invaluable guide to making better advertising. It does not substitute for a creative executional idea. However, it is a means of determining whether the creative idea is saying the right thing to the right person at the right time. It is a way to hold the agency accountable for the effectiveness of the advertising. It is a vital document and must be written prior to every major advertising campaign. It is most effective when written in collaboration with representatives of account management, research, media, creative, and the marketing director of the advertising company. It is not an easy document to write. A great deal of thinking and original research should go into it.

In the remaining part of this chapter we will demonstrate how a creative strategy is written. And we will point out some common mistakes made in its development.

Creative Strategy Form

From data in this chapter, we will work out the strategic thinking process on an actual product. But first, let's take a look at the form—section by section—and emphasize some do's and don'ts.

The Key Fact

The client has come to you with problems concerning his product and company. In order to develop the proper strategy, you must define the key fact or key problem that you as a creative person are trying to solve. This problem

Creative Strategy Development Form

A. THE PROBLEM

    1. The Key Fact
    2. The Marketing Problem Advertising Can Solve

B. THE CREATIVE STRATEGY

    1. What Is the Product?
        Or Service?
        a. In reality?
        b. As perceived?

    2. Who Are the Prospects?
        a. Geographics
        b. Demographics
        c. Psychographics
        d. Media patterns
        e. Buying/use patterns

    3. Who Is the Principal Competition?

    4. What Is the Competitive Consumer Benefit?

    5. What Is the Support for the Benefit? The Reason Why?

    6. The Target Market Incentive Statement

    7. What Is the Tone of the Advertising?

    8. What Is the Communication Objective?
        a. What is the main point?
        b. What action should be taken?

Exhibit 5-1   Creative Strategy Form

must be related to the consumer, since you are not in the business of solving internal organizational dilemmas.

What is the key problem? Stopping declining sales? Introducing a new product? Warding off a price war?

The strategy can only deal with one key fact or problem. It is your job to isolate it and get everyone's agreement that this is indeed the problem you will try to solve.

The Marketing Problem Advertising Can Solve

Several issues must be specified here. First, the marketing problem must flow from the key fact. If the key fact is a declining sales curve, then the statement of the marketing problem must respond to that. For instance, is the marketing problem 1. to get new customers away from competitors, 2. to get present customers to use the product more often, or 3. to attract customers who have never purchased in the product category before?

By distilling all the information you have been given about the client's problem, you are in a position to define the essence of the marketing problem. Let's say that the marketing problem is to get present customers to use the product more often. Now, the question to be asked is "Can advertising solve that problem?"

Maybe, yes. Maybe, no. Take the case of Shredded Wheat cereal. Millions of people buy it, but very few eat it very often. Most eat it about once every two weeks. Can advertising motivate them to use it more often?

If the key fact is that sales are down because distribution is poor, is this a marketing problem advertising can solve? Sometimes, yes. Sometimes, no.

If the key fact is that sales are down because competitors have undercut the price by 20 percent, can advertising solve this marketing problem? Sometimes, yes. Sometimes, no.

To objectively answer this question of "the marketing problem advertising can solve," a great deal of original information and thinking about the vitality of your product in relation to the state of the market is mandatory. Very often though, your decision is a judgment call based on your knowledge and experience.

These two points—the key fact and the marketing problem advertising can solve—must be agreed upon and written down to generate insight into the total problem. It must be written, without prejudice, before the actual writing of the strategy statement. Now, let's move on to the strategy itself.

The Creative Strategy

The Product

Reality. In reality, what is the product you are going to sell? What are its ingredients? How is it made? Where is it grown? Who grows it? Who makes it? State real product information—facts—that may give the creative person the key to writing a more persuasive ad.

If you're selling canned peas, try for interesting facts about the product that may help distinguish it from other canned peas. Are the farmers who grow the peas conscientious? What time do they start picking the crop? When do they stop? Is there a special kind of dirt the product is grown in? A special kind of rainfall? An angle of the sun that is most conducive to growing? Do the pickers wear gloves? Are they clean? Are they proud? When is the picking season? What is the price of the product? The package—what's it like? Where is the product bought? Does it taste good? Why?

These are but a few of the questions that should be asked to build the product reality section of the strategy. Leo Burnett once said "There is inherent news in any product—and this can always be found if you dig hard enough into the product—and dig for facts." This inherent news is often enough to set your product apart from the competition. Many times you may think there is nothing special about the product, but deep probing and imaginative questions will often turn up ideas that can lead to creative executions and eventual sales of the product.

It will surprise you to discover how few advertisers really know what their product is all about until they are thoroughly and intelligently questioned. Equally surprising are the differing points of view about the product given by different members of a client organization. They may each have a different— and enlightening—perspective.

The purpose of the product reality section is to obtain all the facts about the product: 1. to lead to a dramatic selling claim and 2. to get common agreement on what the product is, what it does, and how it acts and feels. Even an objective statement of the product's shortcomings should be noted.

In our opinion, knowledge is the energy of creativity. And the first step in building a fund of knowledge is the product itself.

Perception. Perceptions of the product are as important as the reality—often, they are more important. How do people feel about Shredded Wheat? Is it cold, impersonal? Strawy? Healthy? Tasty? Medicinal? Good for kids? A pain to eat? A laxative? Does it provide memories of childhood? Of Mom and Dad? Of Sunday breakfast?

Everyone concerned with the brand you are selling—at the agency and the advertiser—must be aware of how the brand is perceived by the customer or potential customers. Decisions then must be made: Shall advertising build on the positive perceptions? If so, how? Or are the negative perceptions so strong that advertising should attempt, overtly, to turn them around? Or perhaps these negative perceptions are so strong that they simply can't be changed with advertising.

This section of the strategy is vital to understanding the product and how the consumer feels about it. Many times the consumer's perceptions of the product can give you a clue to what the consumer is really looking for in the product. Often this clue can lead to a strong and motivating competitive consumer benefit.

Consumers' perceptions can be hypothesized on the basis of personal experiences. But, if time and money permit, the information should be gathered from quantitative and qualitative research. This research should be conducted among the user group defined in the marketing problem section of the strategy.

Important in this section of the strategy is also the need to briefly describe the perceptions of the product category you are dealing with. For instance, if you are placing Shredded Wheat in the cereal category, you need to find out how people generally feel about the cereal category. Are cereals considered junk foods? Healthy? A necessity? Calorie-ridden? A tradition?

The product section of this strategy does not just happen. It is the result of constant digging and questioning. If it is put together well, it can lead to solutions to the creative challenge—both in strategic positioning and creative execution. Now, on to the customer.

The Customer

Who is the person most likely to buy your product? Age? Income? Education? All the vital statistics are helpful. But, remember, two families living next door to one another can have the exact same demographics, but one family eats no cereal, the other eats Shredded Wheat. Why?

Are their needs and wants at breakfast different? Again, why? What do they do for exercise? Hobbies? How do they relate to cereals? What is their favorite breakfast? How do they shop? When? Do they eat breakfast alone? Do they eat differently on weekends? On vacation? To write a successful ad, you have to know the customer as if he or she were your sister, brother, or mother.

When Ford Motor Company brought out the Mustang, it was directed at people who were 25 to 35 years old and could afford to spend $2,500, in 1964, for a sporty-looking car.

A year after the successful launch of the car, insurance records showed that accidents involving the Ford Mustang were taking place with as many people between the ages of 45 and 65 as between 25 and 35. Ford may have aimed the Mustang at a chronological age segment but actually sold the car to people of all ages: people who "thought young—and wanted a racy sports type of car to help them feel young."

Don't ever stop at the demographics of a customer. Age and income figures never lead to a good advertisement. Size up the customer as if you were selling someone on the retail floor. If you don't have the luxury of records, make your own hypothesis about the customer's life-style and habits. Talk to people you know: ask people in stores how they feel about the product. Use your imagination to determine who would be most likely to use the product. You'd be surprised how close your hunch will be to the real thing.

To summarize, we are writing this strategy to decide what competitive benefit we can offer a target customer to take business away from a competitor, expand our own business by getting people to use our product more often, or open up a whole new category for our product.

So far, we've analyzed the product and the customer. Now, let's look at the competition.

The Competition

Whom are we competing against? What are their strengths? Their weaknesses? What are they offering the consumer—in reality? Perceptually? Are they vulnerable? Are consumers loyal to them? How loyal? What shares of market do each have? How much do they spend on advertising?

You must know the competition in order to compete. In the case of Shredded Wheat, are you competing against tiny Wheat Chex? Or are you competing in the hot cereal category against Cream of Wheat or Oatmeal? Or, perhaps, against vitamin pills? Or are you competing against general cereals like Corn Flakes, Rice Krispies, or Wheaties? Or against bacon and eggs?

Where do you hope to get your business from? Where does your brand have the most leverage by offering the most persuasive competitive benefit?

You have now ascertained what your product is, what the consumer wants, and who the competition is and what they are offering the consumer. Now, how can you take business away from the competition—business that will contribute significant dollar volume to your brand? This leads you to the most important point of the strategy statement—the competitive consumer benefit.

The Competitive Consumer Benefit

If your strategic thinking is correct, the competitive consumer benefit is simply the key to what the consumer wants to hear about your product. It is nothing more than a factual statement based on your product, the consumer, and the competition of what your brand can uniquely offer that will make the consumer's life a bit better or solve one of the consumer's problems.

The competitive benefit must be a single benefit that can be dramatically executed in a 30-second TV commercial, a one-page ad, or a 24-sheet poster. Very often, seasoned professionals, as well as beginners, try to crowd two promises into the benefit statement. This usually results in a chaotic piece of advertising, going off in several confusing directions. It usually communicates little and almost always lacks persuasion.

If you can offer one simple benefit in a believable, persuasive execution, you're well on your way to a sale.

It is vital to remember that the benefit must be competitive. You must make the consumer believe that your product does something better for him than other products he can buy in the competitive category. In other words, the benefit is not competitive if it simply says, "My product gives you good taste."

The benefit must be competitive: "My product tastes better than all other products in the competitive frame."

The competitive benefit must be a benefit—something that solves a consumer problem or makes the consumer's life easier. The consumer, when hearing the benefit, has every right to ask, "What's in it for me?" If the answer is wishy-washy, then it is clearly not a benefit. If the answer is the same as that of other products, then the benefit is not competitive.

Many people have difficulty in distinguishing product features or product attributes from competitive benefits.

A product feature is something a product does—for example, a washing machine with fewer moving parts. But the benefit of "fewer moving parts" is that you will have fewer repair bills—or less worry.

A product attribute is something the product has—for example, a cereal made from whole grain wheat. The competitive benefit is that it gives you

Exhibit 5-2 This ad could have sold hardware and product features. Instead, it sold something busy executives really want. And it distinguished Xerox from the competition.

energy, or makes you feel good about what you put in your body.

You will find that boring advertising is commonly caused by an emphasis on product attributes, which advertisers think consumers are interested in, but in reality, potential customers couldn't care less about.

Again, people buy quarter-inch holes, not quarter-inch drills. Tell consumers how to solve a problem or how to improve their life, and they'll buy your product. Tell them what makes your product tick and they'll click to another channel.

The Support? The Reason Why?

In order for the competitive consumer benefit to be effective, it must be believable to the consumer. First, it must jibe with the consumer's realm of experience. If you tell the consumer that you have a hair cream that will make him look younger, he won't believe you. If you tell a man you have a hammer that will make him an expert carpenter, he'll have a hard time accepting the idea.

The benefit must be relevant to the consumer's needs, wants, and experience. If the benefit of the product is "more energy," is that important to a 12-year-old who has trouble expending his natural energies?

849 Miles From Nome.

You race at night. The track is faster.

You pray for cold. The dogs like it better.

For two weeks you push — 1,049 frozen, brutal miles.

Dick Mackey
Iditarod Winner

Nothing takes the measure of a team like the Iditarod — the last great race on earth.

If mushing across the cold heart of Alaska is the ultimate test of man and dog,

it's also the ultimate test of the bootmaker's craft.

That's why Timberland has chosen the Iditarod to test its boot collection.

Boots that keep you warm, dry and comfortable under the most inhospitable conditions known to man

are tough enough for anything.

Timberland Boots. Tough enough for the Iditarod.

More quality than you may ever need.

Timberland
MORE QUALITY THAN YOU MAY EVER NEED.

Exhibit 5-3 The very look of the ad, its tone and writing style, give the reader a reason to believe the claim.

The benefit must be supported by a set of reasons to cause belief. In other words, as the Leo Burnett agency puts it, the consumer must be given "permission to believe."

The reason to believe, or benefit support, should come out of the product reality. It should be one fact, something the product does that makes the benefit supportable and believable. It should give the consumer permission to believe the benefit.

The support should be specific and brief. For instance, the claim that a washing machine has 28 percent fewer moving parts than any other washer would clearly support the benefit "less repair bills."

The reason "72 percent more prime wheat" clearly supports a competitive benefit of better health or nutrition.

Very often, the reason-why will become the core of the ad or the television commercial because the benefit is implied or obvious. For instance, Timex has demonstrated the reason-why its watch is built well. The benefit, durability, is summed up in the selling line, "takes a lickin' and keeps on tickin'."

The television or print execution itself can lend support or believability to the benefit and give the consumer permission to believe. The writing style should be fresh, without advertising adjectives and clichés; and the pictures should be novel, tell a story, and use real people. These factors can make the difference between credibility and indifference.

Very often, advertisers are faced with a situation in which their products are virtually at parity with competitive products. And, although they may have offered a competitive benefit in their strategy, they have no significant reason-why to support the benefit. In this case, many creative people resort to a unique, fresh, credible execution that separates their product from the competition. The uniqueness and believable tone of the advertising can build the positive perception in the consumer's mind that your product is truly different from the competition.

At this point, the strategy can be summed up—and checked out—with a piece of shorthand we call the Target Market Incentive Statement.

In one sentence, it recaps the whole strategy statement up to this juncture: "To (User Group, (Name of Brand) is the (Product Category) that (Benefit of Brand)."

For instance, if you were selling Shredded Wheat, targeted it against adult breakfast eaters, decided to compete in the cereal category, and wanted to offer a competitive benefit of more nutrition, here is how the Target Market Incentive statement would be written: "To adult breakfast eaters, Shredded Wheat is the brand of cereal that gives you more nutrition than any other cereal."

If you were selling Shredded Wheat to children who use vitamins, decided to compete against bottled vitamins, and wanted to offer a benefit that this vitamin is more fun to take than any other vitamin, here is the way the Target Marketing Incentive statement would read:

"To children who take vitamin pills, Shredded Wheat is the brand of vitamin that is more fun to eat than other vitamins."

Tone

One of the most important ingredients of the strategy statement is the section called "tone," or "personality," or "manner." This section should flow logically from the rationale behind the strategy. It should express the personality that the advertising will give the product, based on the benefit the product is offering, the consumer, and the competition. For example, if the benefit is offering fun to youngsters, obviously the tone of the advertising will not be "scientific." If all competitors are offering fun through animated characters, perhaps the tonality section should state that we must offer fun but must do it differently, for example, with puppets or movie stars.

This section should definitely be written as a point-of-view, not as a dogma for the creative people.

It should be logical. If you are offering a cure for baldness, a serious tone or personality for the product will be in order. If you are selling a woman's cosmetic, perhaps the tone will be fantasy and futuristic. If you are selling a used car, the tone will probably be tough and competitive.

Action Statement

As a result of the strategy and the creative execution that comes from it, what do you want to have happen? At this point, two action statements should be written. First, what is the main point—the one point—you want the consumer to take away from the advertising? That it's cute? Or funny? Or that it tells him what the product can do for him? The main point "take away" should really be the benefit that is contained in the strategy. It should literally fill out the statement. "I should buy this product because. . . ." That, after all, is the intention of the advertising: to offer one persuasive reason why the prospect should purchase the product.

This main point of communication is a basic criterion on which the advertising should be judged. It is a method of holding the advertising agency accountable for the advertising. For, if the ad does not communicate the benefit, then the communication is wasted.

The second action statement that is written at this point is what you want the consumer to do as a result of seeing your advertising.

Do you want the viewer to think more favorably of your product? Fill out a coupon for more information? Buy your product? Tell a friend about it? Here again, measurable criteria can be applied and areas of accountability can be designated.

As stated earlier in this chapter, an advertising strategy as we have outlined it is not to be mechanically filled out. It is a thinking process that logically takes you through the product, the consumer, the competition and should lead you to a meaningful competitive benefit that will then lead to a compelling, persuasive sales message.

An advertising strategy is a document that we've seen work in every category—from small retail stores to major retail chains, from under-a-dollar package-goods products to complex computers. You need not have the resource of a huge agency or advertiser to utilize it. Any thinking person with a knowledge of marketing and sales and a systematic approach can apply it.

Questions

Here are some basic questions to answer before moving on to the next chapter:

1. What is the benefit of your product? What are the attributes? How can you easily tell the difference? Why is this important in making a sale?
2. How can knowledge of the consumer's life-style and usage habits lead to more effective advertising? How important are user demographics in the creation of advertising?
3. Can't you create more original advertising by avoiding the writing of a strategy? Why restrict your thinking—just create, create, create! What good is strategizing if the consumer doesn't pay attention to commercials anyway?
4. Who should be accountable for advertising that is run on the air or in print? The agency? The client? On what basis should each or both be held accountable?
5. How does advertising distinguish one product from another in the consumer's mind? If products were different to begin with, would we need to worry about distinguishing among them? Why not just show the product and tell the consumer what it does?
6. Think of people you know. Think how credible they are as friends, parents, teachers, etc. Then, try to explain the reason-why they earned their credibility with you—for example, their dress, honesty, use of facts, warmth, and popularity.

7. What benefits does soda pop offer you? A particular brand of soda
   pop? Is it a rational benefit—something the product actually does? Or is
   it an emotional benefit—something the product (or advertising) makes
   you feel it does?

Chapter Six

Thinking Through an Advertising Strategy

A new client has come to you with a new product. Let's assume you've never seen this product before. In fact, the client, named Groves Unlimited, has just discovered it. The company calls it an ORANGE.

The Clients's Description of the Product

Here is the client's description of the product. It is typical of the briefing you'll get on any new product.

Groves Unlimited is a newly formed company based in Orlando, Florida that has just developed and patented a new food product. This product, called an ORANGE, is a round citrus fruit that is approximately 4″ in diameter. The ORANGE has a semihard skin or peel that is considered inedible. However, the meat of the fruit, under the skin, is delicious.

Groves Unlimited has tested the product and can claim that one ORANGE supplies the full recommended daily supply of vitamin C and niacin, as determined by the Food and Drug Administration. The meat of the ORANGE can be eaten directly. It is best eaten in its raw state. It is good at room temperature or refrigerated. It is also possible to squeeze the juice from the ORANGE to make a beverage that requires no sweetening.

Pricing: Groves Unlimited plans to distribute the ORANGE with a recommended list price of $.49/lb. This is approximately $.08 to $.10 per ORANGE.

Packaging: The ORANGE will be sold in single units (loose) or prepackaged in plastic or net sacks with approximately 3 lbs. or 5 lbs. per sack.

Distribution: Groves Unlimited will initially introduce the ORANGE to retail food stores throughout the United States and recommend that it be sold in their produce sections.

Promotion: Groves Unlimited has asked us to create an advertising campaign using radio, television, and consumer magazines to promote the use of this product. The company would like our recommendations on the most likely target market and product segment.

The Assignment

The client has given us his thoughts, and we the agency have an assignment: Initially, we would like to create a strategy for the ORANGE. From this, we will develop an ad campaign as requested by the client.

Key Fact: As you will recall from chapter 5, the strategy begins with the statement of the key fact. What do you think is the key fact from all that you now know about this product? (Remember, you've never heard of the ORANGE before.) Is it that Grove wants to make millions? Or will the orange establish a new taste trend for America? Or is it a discovery that will shake the earth?

The key fact is simply this: There is a new product called the ORANGE and the world has never heard of it.

The Marketing Problem That Advertising Can Solve: Now, the question is: Is this a marketing problem that advertising can solve? The answer, obviously, is yes. The product seems right, the price is right, distribution will be achieved, and advertising should help sell it. But ask yourself—should we go after present users of citrus fruit? Try to expand the category? Or get into a new category? Obviously, there are no current users of our own product to pursue. So, for the purposes of this illustration, let's write the marketing problem statement like this: To get new users to try this product by offering a competitive consumer benefit.

The Product

Now, let's look at the product. In reality, what is it?

The Product—Real: List the most important features of the product:

1. Round fruit with thick skin and juicy meat
2. Tastes slightly sour—slightly sweet
3. Satisfies your thirst
4. Has vitamin C (healthy)
5. Has the same color as the sun
6. Good at breakfast or as a snack
7. Mixes well with alcohol
8. Tasty ingredient for other recipes

We've briefly listed some of the important attributes of the product. Perhaps you can list more. There are some negative features of the product, and they, too, should be listed:

1. Skin tastes awful
2. Too many seeds
3. Sloppy—squirts when cutting
4. More expensive than other fruits, like grapefruit

The Product—Perceived: In this section, we deal with the perceptions of the product. Usually, you would conduct some research to find out what potential consumers think and feel about the product before and after they use it. Let's hypothesize some perceptions—both positive and negative. Add as many as you see fit:

Positive:

1. Better tasting than lemons
2. Pretty—has color of the sun
3. Healthy, natural food with vitamins

Negative:

1. Hard to get open
2. Seedy
3. Hard to get juice out
4. Not as good tasting as milk

The Customer

Now, take a look at the customer. Let's establish some easy, though arbitrary, demographics:

Age: 25–45 years old
Sex: Female
Household Income: $70,000
Education Level: H.S. +

How do you build a campaign on these statistics? You have to know more about the customer. What does she do for a living? Does she love her kids? Her job? Does she work long hours? Does she feel guilty about working and being away from her children? Her husband? Does she wish she had more time to prepare meals? How can the orange solve her problems or make her life easier?

Let's put down in a simple paragraph some information about this woman's life-style and what she may want from the product:

We are targeting the woman who chooses to work but still feels devoted to her family. She is always looking for new ideas in meals, snacks, entertainment, and decorating that will please her family and still be convenient to her schedule.

The Competition

Now, who is our competition for the orange? Where will we get our business from? A snap judgment will say we'll get it from other citrus fruits, like grapefruit and lemon. But why those old standbys? People have been using and drinking them for years. And they're loyal. Can we take business away from these established products? What benefit will people believe makes our product better? Does the world need another citrus fruit? Is there another category we can compete in successfully? Why not against cereals? Or vitamins? Let's list the main forms of competition for the orange, as if it were a new product today:

1. Product Class: Breakfast Juice
   Brand Names: Grapefruit Juice
                  Prune Juice
                  Tomato Juice

2. Product Class: Cereals
   Brand Names: Rice Krispies
                   Total
                   Cap'n Crunch

3. Product Class: Vitamins
   Brand Names: One-A-Day
                   Therm-a-Gard
                   Flintstones

4. Product Class: Snack Foods
   Brand Names: Twinkies
                   Milky Way
                   Fritos

5. Product Class: Decorative Accessories
   Brand Names: Candelabra
                   Vases
                   Horn of Plenty

6. Product Class: Alcoholic Beverages
   Brand Names: Bloody Mary
                   Gimlet
                   Martinis

In which competitive frame should we compete? In which product category can we make the most money? Which is most vulnerable to this new product entry? Let's consider what our new product is and the strengths and weaknesses of all the competitors. Then, let's consider the needs and wants of our target consumer and determine whether our product—the ORANGE—can uniquely and competitively solve her problem or make her life easier.

The Strategy

As we said earlier, this woman would welcome a product that provides new ideas in meals, snacks, entertainment, and decorating—a product that will please her family and still be convenient to her schedule.

Knowing this woman and what she wants, you must ask yourself: Why let the orange compete in a tight, competitive category against other juices or cereals or vitamins? Why not open a whole new category for your product alone and provide this competitive consumer benefit:

The orange makes you feel like a more caring mother and wife than if you used any other combination of products.

The reason-why—or support—could be stated this way:

Works different ways to make your family's life better, easier, and happier. Dozens of innovative ways to use the product: quick snack, breakfast food, table decoration, furniture polish, meal ingredient, cold drink, beverage mixer, vitamin source, and more.

Target Market Incentive: The incentive for the target market could be stated,
To mothers of young families, the ORANGE is a citrus fruit that makes them seem more caring than if they used a combination of other products.
Tone Statement: The tone or personality, of the advertising will, of course, flow from the benefit statement and dramatize it in the context of the target customer.
The tone statement in the strategy could read as follows:
Highly emotional—allows the wife and mother to feel like a heroine to her husband and kids. She's the smart one who discovered this new product.
Action Statement: Now, the *Action Statement.* What do we want the consumer to do as a result of our advertising?

1. Think that she is a more caring mother if she uses ORANGES instead of other products in meals.
2. Buy our product and use it in different ways each day.

Suggestions

When given this hypothetical problem, most people would probably set up the orange as a citrus drink competitive with grapefruit and tomato juice. While this positioning may be sound, the idea behind the exercise is to illustrate how the strategy opens your mind to other ways of selling. It gives you the opportunity to objectively analyze the product, the needs of the customer, and the entry positions into the market. It further gives you the opportunity to be creative in your strategic thinking. By not accepting the obvious course, you may open a market that gives you much more leverage to compete in and is much more lucrative.

Creative Strategy Development Form for THE ORANGE

A. THE PROBLEM

   1. The Key Fact:
      There is a new product called the ORANGE and the world has never heard of it.

   2. The Marketing Problem Advertising Can Solve: To get new users to try this product by offering a competitive consumer benefit.

B. THE CREATIVE STRATEGY

   1. What Is the Product?

a. In reality?	b. As perceived?
1. Round fruit with thick skin and juicy meat	1. Better tasting than lemons
2. Tastes slightly sour—slightly sweet	2. Pretty—has color of the sun
3. Satisfies your thirst	3. Healthy, natural food with vitamins
4. Has vitamin C (healthy)	4. Hard to get open
5. Has the same color as the sun	5. Seedy
6. Good at breakfast or as a snack	6. Hard to get juice out
7. Mixes well with alcohol	7. Not as good tasting as milk
8. Tasty ingredient for other recipes	
9. Skin tastes awful	
10. Too many seeds	
11. Sloppy—squirts when cutting	
12. More expensive than other fruits, like grapefruit	

   2. Who Are the Prospects?
      25–45 year-old females with household incomes above $70,000 and with more than a high school education. We are targeting the woman who chooses to work but still feels devoted to her family. She is always looking for new ideas in meals, snacks, entertainment, and decorating that will please her family and still be convenient to their schedule.

   3. Who Is the Principal Competition?
      No direct competition for our benefit. A number of products would be needed to provide all the benefits of the orange.

   4. What Is the Competitive Consumer Benefit?
      The orange makes you feel like a more caring mother and wife than if you used any other combination of products.

   5. What Is the Support for the Benefit? The Reason Why?
      Works different ways to make your family's life better, easier, and happier. Dozens of innovative ways to use the product: quick snack, breakfast food, table decoration, furniture polish, meal ingredient, cold drink, beverage mixer, vitamin source, and more.

   6. The Target Market Incentive Statement:
      To mothers of young families, the ORANGE is a citrus fruit that makes them seem more caring than if they used a combination of other products.

   7. What Is the Tone of the Advertising?
      Highly emotional—allow the wife and mother to feel like a heroine to her husband and kids. She's the smart one who discovered this new product.

   8. What Is the Communication Objective?
      a. What is the main point?
         Think that she is a more caring mother if she uses ORANGES instead of other products in meals.
      b. What action should be taken?
         Buy our product and use it in different ways each day.

Exhibit 6-1 The final strategy statement is clear and concise.

In addition, as you can see, the strategy statement gives the creative people a clear, sharp course to pursue. In no way does it inhibit creativity. In fact, in our opinion, it encourages it. The strategy gives the creative person a depth of knowledge that can only help lead to more effective ideas. It also narrows the avenues of pursuit and lets the creative person spend his valuable time searching for uniqueness in a given area. The strategy also provides an excellent way to measure the selling power of the creative execution and gives you criteria for evaluating the advertising.

Questions

Before we move on to the creative implementation of the strategy, let us ask a few questions that will let you flex your creative muscles:

1. Think of three unique ways of executing the ORANGE strategy—one, in a magazine ad; two, in a 30-second commercial; three, on an outdoor poster.
2. If you were to do a testimonial commercial to execute the ORANGE strategy, name a personality you would use to deliver the testimonial.
3. If you were to include a demonstration in the execution of the ORANGE strategy, what key point would you demonstrate?
4. What other ways could you write the tone section of the orange strategy that would create different personalities for the product?
5. Given the product, competitive, and customer sections of the strategy, what other benefit statements would be appropriate? And what reason-why statements could be used to support them?

Chapter Seven

From Strategy to Execution: The Art of Creativity

What Creative Advertising Is

Creative advertising is advertising that is created for a specific customer. It is advertising that understands and thinks about the customer's needs. It is advertising that communicates a specific benefit. It is advertising that pinpoints a specific action that the consumer takes. Good advertising understands that people do not buy products—they buy product benefits. Creative advertising does all of the above and, above all, gets noticed and remembered, and gets people to act.

That's the genius of creativity. Not only must you deliver the benefit, but you must do it with showmanship, drama, and excitement so that your advertising breaks through the clutter, avoids the zippers and zappers, gets noticed, gets remembered, and, most important, makes a sale.

Practically everyone is familiar with the advertising campaign for Dr Pepper. (See Exhibit 7-1.) Its strategy delivers the competitive benefit that you can be an independent person, not one of the crowd, when you drink Dr Pepper. The reason-why is that Dr Pepper is not just another sweet cola or citrus drink. It's a special flavor for people who want to be different.

The Dr Pepper strategy is sharp and single-minded. It delivers an emotional benefit of independence and the rational benefit of unique taste. It has isolated a specific target audience. It understands that audience.

The Dr Pepper commercial execution of that strategy could have been dull and straightforward, like this:

Announcer: Hey, kids, are you tired of being one of the crowd? One of those people who always drink the same sweet cola drinks? Or, those

Exhibit 7-1   Dr Pepper

yellow citrus drinks? Break away! Be your own person. Be a
Pepper-upper. A Pepper-upper is his own person! He knows how to
enjoy life! Be a pepper-upper!

That commercial, which, of course, never ran, is accurately on strategy.
However, it is dull and pendantic. It does not empathize with the target audience. It does not dramatize the benefit. It definitely is not memorable or persuasive. It is a turn-off. Compare it to the kind of commercial that actually ran
for Dr Pepper. (See Exhibit 7-2.)

This commercial is on strategy and delivers the benefit, but is so much
more. It stunningly stands out in a sea of ordinary advertising. It is memorable, singable. It tells the target audience, ''We understand you; we know you
and what you want; Dr Pepper is your kind of drink!''

Think of it in economic terms. The dull commercial costs, in media dollars,
exactly the same to run as the exciting commercial. But look at the difference
in voltage, in sheer selling power!

Then, the question is, why is so much advertising dull? Why isn't it more
creative?

What Creative Advertising Isn't

Perhaps it is appropriate to try and define what outstanding creativity is. Is
it sheer bigness? There is a recent Big Mac commercial for McDonald's that
you might have seen. (See Exhibit 7-3.) The commercial shows a two-story
high Big Mac. Sitting on top of the latex creation is a real grand piano—with a
man-in-the-moon look-alike at the keyboard. He croons for McDonald's,

BOY: Hey Patty, what's it take to be a Pepper?
PATTY: It's easy.

PATTY (Singing): To be a Pepper, original like a Pepper, all you gotta do is taste.

SINGERS: Be a Pepper

To know the pleasure of a flavor you will treasure

All you gotta do is taste.
Be a Pepper.

The flavor's got a feeling, original and appealing, and all you gotta do is taste.

To be a Pepper, open up a Dr Pepper, and all you gotta do is taste.

The more you pour it
The more you will adore it
All you gotta do is taste.

To be a Pepper
Open up a Dr Pepper
All you gotta do is taste.

Be a Pepper, drink Dr Pepper.
Be a Pepper, drink Dr Pepper, yeah.

Exhibit 7-2   Dr Pepper storyboard

MAC: WHEN THE CLOCK STRIKES

MAC: HALF PAST SIX

MAC: BABE

MAC: TIME TO HEAD FOR

MAC: GOLDEN LIGHTS

MAC: IT'S A GOOD TIME

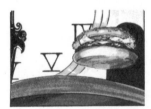

MAC: FOR THAT GREAT TASTE

MAC: DINNER

MAC: AT MCDONALD'S

MAC: IT'S MAC TONIGHT

MAC: COME ON MAKE IT MAC TONIGHT

Exhibit 7-3   An award-winning commercial for McDonald's.

1. (MUSIC UNDER) AIR TRAFFIC CONTROLLER: Roger, Manhattan,

2. continue to descend to flight level eight zero.

3. PILOT: (VO) Roger, ... descending to F-L-8 zero. (SFX: DOG BARKS)

4. (MUSIC AND SFX: DOG WHINES)

5. (MUSIC)

6. AIR TRAFFIC CONTROLLER: Roger, Manhattan, continue to 2000 feet,

7. reduce speed to 1-7-0 knots.

8. ANNCR: (VO) Every year, more people

9. choose to fly with British Airways,

10. to more countries than with any other airline.

11. (SFX: RUMBLE)

12. (SFX)

13. AIR TRAFFIC CONTROLLER: Manhattan, this is ...

14. leaving 2000 feet on the flight path.

15. ANNCR: (VO) In fact, every year we bring more people across the Atlantic than the entire population of Manhattan.

16. AIR TRAFFIC CONTROLLER: Manhattan, you are clear to land.

17. (MUSIC AND SFX: RUMBLE)

18. ANNCR: (VO) British Airways,

19. the world's favourite airline.

20. (SFX: LASER)

Exhibit 7-4   An award-winning commercial created by Saatchi & Saatchi in London.

while his 10-pound head rotates 360 degrees. Exhibit 7-4 shows another example of bigness, this time from British Airways.

Does bigness in itself make a sale? Is it creativity? Or is it simply a way to gain recognition for a product attribute?

Is outstanding creativity the use of high-powered personalities to deliver selling points? Companies today are spending millions of dollars for stars like Michael Jackson, Lionel Ritchie, and Michael J. Fox. Bill Cosby, who receives approximately one million dollars per commercial, is now the spokesman for E.F. Hutton, Jell-O, and Eastman Kodak. Is this creativity? Or is it just an expensive method of achieving memorability?

Is creativity the use of exciting musical scores that rival or beat the production values of Broadway and Hollywood? Certainly music sets a mood and personality for the product, but in itself, is it strong enough to deliver a compelling sales message? Too often we are overwhelmed with mood and entertainment and wonder what the commercial is trying to say.

Is creativity the use of "life-style" photography that dramatically and graphically portrays the user of the product in real-life situations? These types of commercials, done for many retail chains and alcohol products, are usually brilliant pieces of film. They enable the potential consumer to identify with the product or the store being advertised. These commercials may be interesting to watch, but very often, they do not separate one brand from another. They are usually distinguished only by expertise in casting and excellence in direction. They often say little about the product being advertised.

Is the spending of millions of dollars on commercial production the answer to getting through to the consumer? Is the consumer impressed with flash, splash, and larger-than-life drama, or is the consumer interested in ideas that demonstrate how the product helps solve a problem or makes life easier?

The Big Idea

In our opinion, a creative ad or commercial starts with an idea that uniquely dramatizes or demonstrates the competitive benefit.

An idea is not someone standing or sitting and talking at you. An idea is not two women meeting in a supermarket or at a Laundromat. An idea is not an arrow or finger pointing at product features. Nor is it a talking refrigerator.

An idea is a set of words in combination with a picture or a series of pictures that dramatizes what a product will do for you. Showing a beautiful woman with radiant hair and asking the provocative question "Does she or doesn't

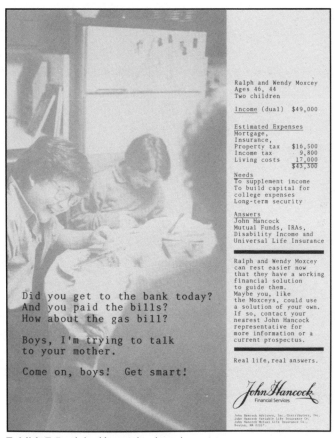

Exhibit 7-5 John Hancock print ad.

she?''—and answering, ''Hair so natural, only her hairdresser knows for sure''—that's an idea. Showing two ex-sports heroes arguing whether Miller Lite is good because it's less filling or because it tastes good, and ending with the surprising line ''Everything you've ever wanted in a beer—and less''— that's an idea. Creating a world called Marlboro Country and populating it with rugged cowboys—that's an idea. Campaign lines like ''Brylcreem, a little dab'll do ya,'' Avis's ''We're only Number Two,'' ''Hertz puts you in the driver's seat,'' ''Which twin has the Toni?''—those are ideas.

Fresh visuals and people like fictional Bartles and James, using ''real people'' language to tell their story—that's an idea.

Effective advertising ideas can utilize bigness, personalities, great production, outstanding music, or none of the above. A big idea can be as simple as John Hancock's unique way of selling life insurance in print and TV (see Exhibits 7-5 and 7-6).

VISUAL	AUDIO

Sam Ostroff
Barbara Tiner

Ages 31, 27
Single

B: (Opens a fortune cookie)
"Be fruitful and multiply"
(Both Laugh)

Income
Salaries:
Sam $28,000
Barbara 30,000

Savings/Investments:
Sam $3,100
Barbara 7,000

S: You know apart from the fact that
we love each other and we know
we can live together...it makes
sense from a financial point also.

Needs
Consider advantages of joint financial
strategy

B: Is that how you see it?

S: No. No...it's just that along with
everything else there's that as well.

B: I don't know. You make it sound
like...a merger or something.

Answers
John Hancock Variable Life
John Hancock Tax Exempt Mutual
   Funds
John Hancock Disability Income

S: All I meant is that we wouldn't need
two cars...two apartments...two of
everything. That's all I meant.

B: Silence

Real life, real answers.
John Hancock Financial Services

S: Let's just forget that. Um. The
important thing is...is that we love
each other...and ...

Exhibit 7-6 Another John Hancock advertisement. In a simple, unassuming way, John Hancock has broken the mold of insurance ads that portray little more than corporate symbols.

CUST. #1: It certainly is a big bun.
CUST. #2: It's a very big bun.

CUST. #1: A big fluffy bun.

CUST. #2: It's a very...big...fluffy...
bun.

CUST. #3: Where's the beef?
ANNCR: Some hamburger places give
you a lot less beef on a lot of bun.

CUST. #3: Where's the beef?

ANNCR: At Wendy's, we serve a hamburger we modestly call a "Single" —
and Wendy's Single has more beef
than the Whopper or Big Mac. At
Wendy's, you get more beef and less
bun.

CUST. #3: Hey, where's the beef? I
don't think there's anybody back
there!

ANNCR: You want something better,
you're Wendy's Kind of People.

Exhibit 7-7   "Where's the beef?" became a household expression, but it also sold hamburgers
for Wendy's.

In order to create "big ideas," you must first have the ability to recognize one. A big idea is an idea that dramatizes or demonstrates how the product benefits the consumer. It usually stems from a specific product advantage—for example, the Wendy's commercial in which Clara Peller asked, "Where's the beef?" This commercial came from a strategy that said the consumer wants more beef, because that's why he or she buys hamburgers in the first place. The commercial brilliantly dramatizes the strategy (see Exhibit 7-7). The famous Rice Krispies advertising is a big idea that has worked for 50 years. "Snap, Crackle & Pop" dramatizes a product attribute that simply translates into a meaningful and competitive consumer benefit.

Another prerequisite for creating a big idea is the desire to do it. Going for a big idea means that you don't accept the first, the second, or even the tenth idea that comes along. Despite the deadlines, you dedicate the manpower, the time, and the sweat until you come up with an original, disarming, memorable piece of communication.

The third requirement for a big idea is climate—both within the agency and especially at the advertiser. There must be a total respect for—including support and encouragement of—the creative person's instinct and judgment. Oscar Wilde once said, "An idea that doesn't make you nervous is not an idea at all." That is particularly true in advertising, where the production and dissemination of ideas can cost millions and millions of dollars.

Questions

It would be beneficial to familiarize yourself with advertising executions in various media. Here are some questions to consider:

1. Select five of your favorite TV commercials and try to figure out why you like them. Do they adhere to the definition of effective advertising presented in this book?
2. Select five magazine ads and, without reading the body copy, ascertain the consumer benefit. Do you think the benefits are competitive? Are they meaningful to the target consumer? Who is the target consumer?
3. Name one commercial you've seen in the past week that you think represents a big idea. Why does it? What is the benefit the product delivers?
4. Try to derive the strategy from a TV commercial you like. Write it down. Then create a 60-second radio commercial from the written strategy.

Chapter Eight

How to Judge
an Advertising Execution

In the United States, approximately 60 billion dollars are spent each year in national advertising. Yet, in every poll we've seen people say that about 75 percent of all advertising is dull, boring, sleep inducing.

No basic rules can prevent advertising from being uninteresting. However, there are some basic guidelines that can help. We call these the *Seven Deadly Sins* and the *Seven Heavenly Virtues*. If you avoid the former and embrace the latter, you are sure to score much higher with today's cynical viewer or reader.

The Seven Deadly Sins

The first sin, advertising the advertiser, concerns itself with messages the advertiser wants to hear rather than messages the consumer wants to hear. It usually is headlined by a bombastic claim—set in large type—that says something like "We stand for Quality!" or "We're proud of our record!" This type of ad is commonplace. It is usually written by lazy writers or by egotistical advertisers who only care about themselves. The consumer has every right to ask, "Who cares about your quality or your record? What are you going to do for me—today?"

The type of ad that represents the second deadly sin, making exaggerated, unbelievable claims, typically leaves readers or viewers incredulous and ill-disposed to buying the product. You've seen or heard the lines "(Brand Name), over all the rest"; "The greatest thing to come out of a pump since water"; "Quite simply, the best"; or, "When you make the most advanced soap, what do you do for an encore?" It is almost a rule: the less information and the less salesmanship contained in the ad, the more numerous and inflated its adjectives.

We call the third deadly sin the "one foot plus teeth" syndrome. The people in the ads guilty of this sin are always standing within one foot of one another and are always smiling. They don't talk, act, or look like real people. They wink at you. They slap each other on the back. They say, "Gollee" and "Wow!" when they see the product. The things they care, worry, or seem enthusiastic about are entirely contrived. They usually reflect the demographic definition of the target audience—even to the point of showing the 1.2 children and the family dog.

The fourth deadly sin involves Art for Art's Sake and Copy for Tom's Sake. Art is the art director, and Tom is the copy writer. And they commit this sin because they are frustrated artists. Both attempt to create ads or commercials with elaborate pictures or drawings and tons of high-blown rhetoric. Everything in an ad should be functional. Nothing should call attention to the mechanics of the ad, for example, showing the main illustration upside down. Good graphics and a good headline, not a showy display of the creative person's skills, should work together to persuade the reader that the product is worthwhile.

The fifth deadly sin is following the leader. We see it over and over again. Somebody gets a great idea for an ad. Then somebody else says: "Hey, that's a great idea. Let's do something like it." And they do. And then somebody else copies them. And, then again, somebody else copies them. This sin is most often evidenced in cigarette, beer, and soft drink advertising, when people are fearful of changing the look of the category. It's a truism in advertising—imitation is the sincerest form of boredom.

It is a widespread belief in advertising that hard sell means battering down the consumer's resistance—torturing him so much that he'll say uncle and buy your product. This kind of advertising, representing the sin of Intimidation, or The Hard-Sell Fallacy, is evidenced by pile-driver layouts with mammoth type in print and loud, shouting announcers on TV. Often you'll hear so-called selling lines loudly repeated, ad nauseum. The hardest selling of all is gentle persuasion. Overwhelming rhetoric does not replace ideas or information.

There is a certain kind of advertiser, or creative person, who assumes that the consumer will believe anything. The Arrogant Advertiser who makes this assumption is guilty of the seventh deadly sin. This follower of Barnum's claim that "there's a sucker born every minute" will propose the preposterous, exaggerate the truth, and overwrite in an attempt to overwhelm. However, it has been proven, time and again, that advertising is accepted by individuals only if it agrees with their experience or common sense. The age of baloney has gone the way of the medicine man.

The Seven Heavenly Virtues

Having put to rest the Seven Deadly Sins, let's move to some of the principles that can lead to more effective advertising: the Seven Heavenly Virtues.

The first heavenly virtue in all advertising is to deliver a significant, competitive promise or benefit. This promise may be either rational, emotional, or a combination of both. It must, *must* come out of the product. It can be depicted in words, a picture, or ideally, in both. Exhibit 8-1 shows a perfect example of a promise explicitly and effectively delivered in a magazine spread. The promise may be implied by the tone and substance of the ad, as it is in Exhibit 8-2. Or it may be dramatized by an involving "story" that is inviting to read as it is in Exhibit 8-3.

Every brand has what we call a personality bank, which is the basis of the second heavenly virtue. In this bank are stored the perceptions of the brand—its personality. Everytime you run a dull, offensive, or misleading ad, you make a withdrawal from the personality bank. Even when you come out with an inferior extension, you make a withdrawal. Every piece of communication, including advertising and sales promotion, should make a deposit in the personality bank instead of a withdrawal. Every ad should be designed to build a long-term personality that is always welcome in the consumer's home, that almost makes the advertising and the brand part of his or her life. (See Exhibit 8-4.)

To follow the third heavenly virtue, be specific. Pin things down, present evidence—facts—and the consumer will reward you. Don't ever be too lazy to dig for the specifics. Don't ever be too complacent to present them in a fresh, uncomplicated way. Specifically back up your promise, and you cement a sale. Exhibit 8-5 shows how specific facts support an emotional appeal.

In our opinion, the greatest art directors and copywriters are masters of the art of omission, that is, their work represents the fourth heavenly virtue, simplicity. The consumer is interested in only one thing: "What's in it for me?" Tell them—be brief and be gone. That's the secret of good ad making. As evidenced in Exhibit 8-6, three words

Exhibit 8-1   A simple promise, brilliantly delivered.

Exhibit 8-2   Just the feel and look of this ad for Snickers delivers the promise in a memorable way.

Exhibit 8-3   Proof, again, that good advertising need not be dull.

WITH A HAIRCUT in Lynchburg, Tennessee, you get a lot of conversation and a lot less hair.

J. C. Riddle is as proud of Jack Daniel's Distillery as anyone here in the Hollow. So visitors in need of barbering hear a lot about the age-old charcoal mellowing process our founder perfected in 1866 and we still insist upon to this day. By the time folks look in the mirror they know two things for sure: nobody ever made whiskey like Jack Daniel. And nobody ever cut hair like J. C. Riddle.

CHARCOAL
MELLOWED
◊
DROP
◊
BY DROP

Tennessee Whiskey • 90 Proof • Distilled and Bottled by Jack Daniel Distillery
Lem Motlow, Prop. Route 1, Lynchburg (Pop. 361) Tennessee 37352
Placed in the National Register of Historic Places by the United States Government

Exhibit 8-4 A personality should reflect and help dramatize the benefit of the product.

Exhibit 8-5 Even an emotional appeal becomes more persuasive when it's backed up with relevant facts.

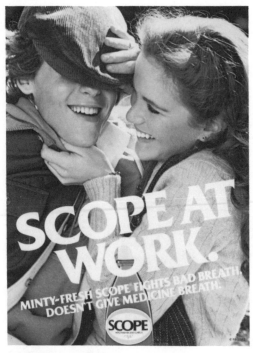

Exhibit 8-6 Good creative people
practice the act of omission.

Exhibit 8-7 How can you help reading
and loving this Hershey Kisses ad?

and one picture can say it all. The Hershey's Kisses ad in Exhibit 8-7 quickly tells the consumer what you're selling in an involving, warm manner.

The fifth heavenly virtue is directness. You have to make your point quickly and unequivocally. To be obscure or oversubtle in advertising is suicide. The average reader spends about a second and a half before he turns the magazine page or tunes out the TV commercial. He does not read copy. He does not remember from one minute to the next what he has seen or read. There is a moment of truth in all advertising in which you either connect or you throw away thousands and thousands of the advertiser's dollars. (See Exhibits 8-8, 8-9, and 8-10 for examples of direct, compelling ads.)

Know your customers. Know your customers. Then, to acquire the next heavenly virtue, make sure the ad talks to these customers in their language and depicts them the way they really are. In Exhibit 8-11, the people who wrote the American Express ad really knew the woman they were addressing. They knew how she shopped, when she shopped, how she dressed, and what she was really like. You don't have to show a picture of the customer to show that you know him or her. In Exhibit 8-12, the advertiser knows the Miracle Whip lover—a person for whom, without Miracle Whip, a sandwich is not a sandwich.

Good advertising embraces all the other virtues and combines them with surprise, the seventh heavenly virtue. Insist on the unusual, the uncommon, the unexpected. Otherwise, the viewer or reader will insist on shutting you out. Make it a rule never to create trite, cliché-ridden advertising just because that's what everybody is doing. Break the category paradigm and you'll break through the clutter. For example, a simple trade ad (Exhibit 8-13) for Heinz Ketchup broke all the rules with an idea you rarely see in trade advertising. Crown Royal and Chevas Regal have also rejected the liquor industry clichés. (See Exhibits 8-14 and 8-15.) And Atmos clocks, in a category that is usually pure fashion, offers a surprising story that is brilliantly written (see Exhibit 8-16).

If you avoid the seven deadly sins and strive for the seven heavenly virtues, you can probably become a master craftsman of advertising. However, there is a higher level of advertising that contains yet another virtue. We discuss it separately because, although it is, like the other elements of good advertising, indispensable to success, it is more a product of inborn talent than of hard work. It can best be described as vitality. It starts as an inspired idea—like the Marlboro Man or "You've come a long way baby"—and it is nurtured by creativity (see Exhibits 8-17

Exhibit 8-8   The message of good advertising as evidenced by this campaign is Be Direct.

Exhibit 8-9   More good, direct advertising.

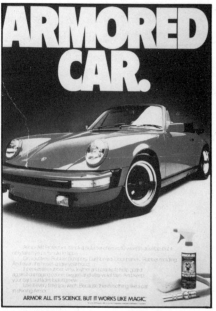

Exhibit 8-10   Still another simple, direct, effective ad.

Exhibit 8-11 American Express
advertisement

Exhibit 8-12 Miracle Whip
advertisement

Exhibit 8-13   Heinz advertisement

Exhibit 8-14   Crown Royal advertisement

Exhibit 8-15   Chivas Regal advertisement

Exhibit 8-16   Atmos advertisement

and 8-18). Year after year it takes on new life and continues to be seen, heard, and remembered.

How Do You Judge Your Own Work?

One of the most difficult positions to be in as an advertising person is to know for certain when the ad you are about to recommend is good or bad. Who knows if you ever know for sure? The toughest aspects of creating an ad are the loneliness and desperation involved in struggling for an idea—especially as a deadline approaches. The question eventually arises: When do you stop working on the ad and start recommending? At what point do you become satisfied? On what criteria do you base that judgment?

These are difficult questions to answer. Many creative people will tell you that they just sense when their ad is right. Many advertisers will tell you they know it when they see it. Many people in the business rely on research to help them in their judgment.

Here are some basic ways you can evaluate an ad or commercial you've created.

Let's assume you've written something you like. It's an idea—an original one. It's direct. It's simple. It seems exciting. But you wonder: Is it really good, or am I just in love with my own work?

In this situation, it's advisable to put the ad or commercial out of your mind for a couple of days. Then, look at it fresh. Does it still measure up to the criteria listed above? If it does, then put it up against some even tougher measurements:

1. Honestly, does the commercial dramatize, illustrate, demonstrate, or depict one thing the product will do for the target audience?
2. Is this one thing the benefit that was stated in the advertising strategy?
3. Will your target audience respond to the commercial by saying, "That's a good ad" or "That's a good product" or both?
4. Judge the selling power of your ad or commercial in the environment of your competitors' advertising. Will your ad still make a sale after the viewer is influenced by your competitors' advertising? Is your advertising more memorable, more persuasive?
5. Is the commercial a friend or foe? Is it in good taste? Is it phoney? Does it sound like an ad? Is it trying to help one person solve a problem? Would the ad or commercial be welcome in your home over and over again?
6. Does the commercial have "grab value"? Do the first five seconds get attention? Do the first five seconds make you want to see and hear more?

Exhibit 8-17 Marlboro's classic advertisement and campaign.

Exhibit 8-18 Virginia Slims advertisement—another memorable image.

7. Are you proud of the ad or commercial? Does it make you feel good? Would you be eager to read it or show it to your mother, husband, or sister?

Questions

In your job in advertising you will probably be responsible for the spending of millions of dollars. Far from a game, advertising is a serious business that, in its mass audience form, has been around for less than 100 years. The astute professional will constantly look for new and better ways to communicate and persuade.

Here are some questions that might help you get there:

1. How can I get to know the consumer in more depth? Can advertising be more selective in talking to the various needs and wants of people?
2. Shouldn't there be a more scientific way to measure the effectiveness of an ad or commercial?
3. Should the selling of a product be left to the imagination of a writer or art director?
4. If simplicity is the key to good advertising, must so much money be spent in the production of advertising?
5. What new other selling techniques could you envision that might improve the uncertainties of current mass advertising?
6. Are emotional advertising appeals a more powerful selling tool than rational appeals?

Photo and Illustration Credits

1–1   Courtesy of the CLIO awards

1–2   Courtesy of the Promotion Marketing Association of America

1–3   Courtesy of Clairol Inc.

1–4   Courtesy of Quaker Oats Company

2–2   © The Perrier Group

2–3   Courtesy of General Foods Corporation

3–1   Adapted with permission from Wilbur Schramm and Donald Roberts, eds., *The Process and Effects of Mass Communication* (Urbana: University of Illinois Press, 1971)

3–4   Courtesy of the William Wrigley Jr. Company

4–1   Adapted from Loudon and Della Bitta, *Consumer Behavior: Concepts and Applications,* 2nd edition (New York: McGraw-Hill, 1984)

4–2   Adapted from A.E. Pitcher's "The Role of Branding in International Advertising," *International Journal of Advertising* (1984,4)

5–2   Courtesy of the Xerox Corporation

5–3   Courtesy of the Timberland Company

7–1   Courtesy of the Dr Pepper Company

7–2   Courtesy of the Dr Pepper Company

7–3   Courtesy of Davis, Johnson, Mogul & Colombatto, Inc. Advertising

7–4   Courtesy of British Airways

7–5   Courtesy of John Hancock Mutual Life Insurance Company, Boston, Massachusetts 02117

7–6   Courtesy of John Hancock Mutual Life Insurance Company, Boston, Massachusetts 02117

7–7   Courtesy of Wendy's International, Inc.

8–1   Courtesy of American Athletic, Inc.

8–2   Courtesy of Mars, Incorporated. Snickers® is a federally registered trademark of Mars, Incorporated.

8–3   Courtesy of United States Army Recruiting

8–4   Courtesy of Jack Daniel Distillery

8–5   Courtesy of the American Cancer Society

8–6   Courtesy of Procter & Gamble Co.

8–7   This Hershey's Kisses advertisement is reprinted by permission of the copyright owner, Hershey Foods Corporation, Hershey, Pennsylvania, U.S.A. The conical configuration, the attached plume device and the words "Hershey's Kisses" are registered trademarks of Hershey Foods Corporation.

Photo and Illustration Credits

TITLES OF INTEREST FROM
NTC BUSINESS BOOKS

Contact: 4255 West Touhy Avenue
Lincolnwood, IL 60646-1975
800-323-4900 (in Illinois, 312-679-5500)

Essentials of Media Planning by Arnold Barban, Steven Cristol, and Frank Kopec

Sales Promotion Essentials by Don Schultz and Bill Robinson

Successful Direct Marketing Methods by Bob Stone

Strategic Advertising Campaigns by Don Schultz, Dennis Martin, and William Brown

How to Produce Effective TV Commercials by Hooper White

Fundamentals of Copy and Layout by Albert Book and Dennis Schick

The Advertising Agency Business by Herbert Gardner

The Dictionary of Advertising by Laurence Urdang

Opportunities in Marketing Careers by Margery Steinberg

Opportunities in Advertising Careers by Bill Pattis